Good Pope John

To John McCaffrey
in friendship

Michael Collins

Good Pope John

A Short Biography

the columba press

Published in 2014 by
the columba press
55A Spruce Avenue,
Stillorgan Industrial Park,
Blackrock, Co. Dublin

Cover design by David Mc Namara C.Ss.R.
Cover image courtesy of Fotografia Felici
Origination by The Columba Press
Printed by Sprint-print Ltd

ISBN 9781 78218 134 7

Table of Contents

Preface

'Think not of your fears but of your unfulfilled dreams. Concern yourself not with what you have tried and failed to do but with what it is still possible for you to do.'

These optimistic words of Pope John XXIII express succinctly the interior spirit of one of the most remarkable religious leaders of our time.

From a small village in northern Italy, Angelo Roncalli rose to be the spiritual leader of the world's Catholics. His warm personality and astute wisdom also gained admirers from other faiths and from those of none.

One of Angelo Roncalli's most endearing characteristics was his lack of vanity and his insatiable curiosity about others. Sitting for an official portrait, he remarked to the photographer that if God had really wanted him to be pope he ought to have made him more photogenic.

Angelo Roncalli was, for most of his life, a conventional Italian cleric. Judged by his superiors to be competent, if not outstanding, he fulfilled a number of important roles before his surprise election to the papacy at the age of seventy-six. Roncalli himself was astonished when his fellow cardinals chose him to succeed Pope Pius XII.

John was garrulous rather than loquacious, shrewd rather than a gifted tactician. Throughout his life he preserved a tenacious loyalty to his family and pride in his native land. Each day he avidly read the regional newspaper *The Bergamo Echo*. Even as pope he had the paper delivered. One morning when his private secretary came to clear the desk and remove the papers, *The Bergamo Echo* was nowhere to be found. The pope had been dismayed about the report of a murder in the district and did not want his staff to see the news.

Angelo Roncalli possessed an enormous talent for making and keeping friends. An extrovert, he kept up an impressive correspondence with family and friends, offering advice and support. This often extended to charity. To mark the fifth anniversary of his mother's death he sent money to the bishop of his home diocese of Bergamo for the poor. While he did not disregard money, he was generous in sharing with people he found in need. In letters and cards exchanged with family and friends for some seventy years, Angelo Roncalli showed his love of gossip for which, in moments of recollection, he often reproached himself. While Roncalli was Apostolic Nuncio in France, Cardinal Suhard of Paris went to Rome to speak with Archbishop Montini, the future Pope Paul VI. The cardinal complained that Roncalli was indiscreet and often talked about candidates for the episcopate.

John's most enduring legacy was the Second Vatican Council which he convened just three months after his election. He could not have foreseen the manner in which the historical gathering would mould the shape of the Church for future generations but he had a historian's grasp of the length of time required for change. While at the beginning he had hoped for a short triumphant Council, he soon understood that the enterprise was far greater and complex than he had originally planned.

As death approached, he bade farewell to his family and friends with the words, 'My bags are packed. I am ready to go.' His death sparked off a genuine outpouring of grief throughout the world.

Some years after his death the cause for his beatification was opened in Rome. The case of the inexplicable healing of Sr Caterina Capitani was accepted for his beatification. At the age of twenty-two and a member of the Congregation of the Daughters of Charity, the Italian Religious was suffering from a severely ulcerated stomach. She claimed to have had a vision of John XXIII at her bedside promising that she would be healed. A series of fourteen operations were necessary, one of which required the removal of most of her stomach. The prognosis left little hope of survival. Her immediate and definitive recovery was judged inexplicable by a panel of medics. Sr Caterina survived and was present at the beatification ceremony in St Peter's Square on 3 September 2003. She died at the age of sixty-eight in 2010, having dedicated her life to work in a hospital caring for the sick.

The cause for canonisation generally requires a second miracle performed after the beatification. In July 2013 Pope Francis announced that he would canonise Blessed Pope John XXIII and Blessed Pope John Paul II in the same ceremony, with the date set as 27 April 2014. In a historic occasion celebrated in St Peter's Square, Pope Francis was joined by emeritus Pope Benedict XVI along with some eight hundred thousand pilgrims. In his homily the pontiff paid tribute to John's openness to the Holy Spirit. 'In convening the Second Vatican Council John XXIII showed an exquisite openness to the Holy Spirit. He let himself be led and he was for the Church a pastor, a servant and leader. This was his great service to the Church; he was the pope of openness to the Holy Spirit.'

But for most who remembered the cheerful smiling Angelo Roncalli, he would remain forever in their hearts as Good Pope John.

CHAPTER ONE

IN THE SHADOW OF THE MOUNTAIN

In the mid-morning of Friday, 25 November 1881, cries were heard in the bedroom of Giovanni Battista Roncalli and his wife Marianna. Rain had beaten down incessantly on the roof tiles since dawn. Autumn that year had turned into a frigid winter.

After nine months, Marianna's pregnancy was over. The midwife encouraged her in the last few moments while women from the town busied themselves bearing water into the room and preparing blankets for the new baby.

Giovanni stood anxiously outside the bedroom. He and Marianna had been childhood friends and had married when they were both twenty-three. One of the women came out of the bedroom to tell Giovanni the news. His first son had been born.

Already the parent of three girls, Giovanni had hoped for a son, one who would help him in the future to farm the patch of land rented on the plains of Sotto il Monte, seven miles northeast of Bergamo, in northern Italy. The sturdy stone farmhouse was built around two courtyards cluttered with carts and farming implements. The family rented eight acres of land. The annual crop was shared between the Roncalli family and the landlords while the family relied on four cows for their dairy needs. The daily meal consisted largely of a cornmeal called polenta and various forms of fowl and game.

To further supplement the family income, the Roncallis kept silkworms. The silk was separated in a lower storeroom on the ground floor and was sold to traders to be woven into fine fabrics.

In the afternoon the infant was taken to the local church of Santa Maria di Brusicco for baptism. It was the tradition of the diocese of Bergamo at the time to christen children almost as soon as they were born. The family had to wait for the priest to return from visitation.

When he arrived in the late afternoon the local parish priest, Don Francesco Rebuzzini, performed the brief ceremony in Latin. Zaverio, the child's grand-uncle, stood as godfather. In an age of high infant mortality, baptism was seen as a spiritual passport to paradise. The godparents also played a significant role. If one or both parents were incapacitated or died, godparents were expected to adopt the child and provide accommodation, food and primary education. After the ceremony, the priest recorded the birth and details of the family in long copperplate handwriting.

That evening the family gathered around the table in the kitchen to share a meal together. Three generations were represented in the small room looking out onto the courtyard of the house. Afterwards the family knelt to recite the rosary. In their prayers they gave thanks to God for the birth of little Angelo Giuseppe.

The Roncalli family had a long history in the region of Bergamo. A document from 1288 mentions Ser Bonadeo de la Roncaia di San Giovanni Bianco. By 1303 another document modifies the name to Della Roncallia. One branch of the family became merchants while the other cultivated the land.

Uncle Zaverio was to play an important part in Angelo's life. The Roncalli household consisted of two brothers whose families shared the house. Zaverio, although unmarried, was acknowledged as the patriarch of the household. In disputes all were expected to submit to his judgement. In later life Pope John was to recall his family as 'somewhat unsophisticated and taciturn, but good Christians all the same'. When Angelo was just two years old, his six-year-old sister Maria Caterina died.

Angelo's very first memory of his childhood was recalled by the elderly John XXIII while receiving a group in audience at the Vatican. He recounted that one birthday his mother took him to the local church of Santa Maria delle Caneve.

The church was so crowded that when Marianna and her six little children arrived they had to wait outside. The sounds of hymns wafted out through the open doorway. The young Angelo (called Angelino by his mother), was impatient to see what was inside. His mother lifted him to the window. As he cupped his hands and peered wide-eyed through the frosty glass, his mother murmured. 'See how beautiful the Madonna is?' Angelino was four years old. The following year Angelo was enrolled in the local school, moving three years later into a newly-established state school.

As the nineteenth century drew to a close, Italy underwent enormous changes. The population during Angelo's early childhood was approximately twenty-nine million. Italy had been declared unified only in 1861, having for centuries previously been divided into city states, duchies, republics and kingdoms. The economy was largely agricultural while industry was confined to the larger cities. More than sixty-five per cent of the population lived on the land. Close on two hundred thousand Italians migrated each year to other parts of Europe and to the New World. The most widespread cause of illness was malnutrition. One-fifth of children born died before their first birthday.

The Italian language had not fully emerged from the variety of dialects spoken throughout the land. Part of the great nineteenth-century struggle for unification was to improve education and eliminate poverty. The enterprise was occasionally violent, slow and achieved only in part.

Tragedy struck Roncalli's family once more in March 1888 when Angelo's infant brother of three weeks died suddenly. At the age of seven, Angelo was confirmed by the Bishop of Bergamo, Monsignor Camillo Guindani, and received his First Holy Communion. This was unusually young for the time. Recalling the event in his twilight years, Angelo Roncalli recollected that he was given the task of compiling the list of his companions in a pious association, the Apostleship of Prayer. 'This was the first writing exercise I recall. It was the first page of so many that would proliferate in half a century of living with pen in hand.'

Don Francesco was an important influence on the young Angelo's life, having been parish priest since 1872. Along with other boys of the parish, Angelo served Mass and assisted at baptisms, weddings and funerals. This introduced him to the richness of the Church's liturgical year.

Parish life consisted of daily and Sunday Mass as well as pious devotions which took place on feast days and usually in the early evening. Families gathered in the church for novenas, Benediction of the Blessed Sacrament and litanies which marked out the feast days of the saints.

Each evening after supper, most families gathered in the kitchens of their homes to recite the Rosary. Angelo Roncalli was to remain steadfast in the childhood piety which he learned at home and in his parish.

In later life, Pope John confessed that there was never a time when he did not want to be a priest. He mentioned his wish to Don Francesco Rebuzzini one day following the morning Mass when he was about seven. Although it was common at the time for young boys to enter the Junior Seminary, Don Francesco gave him little encouragement.

'This collar', said the priest, 'is not easy to wear and cuts the throat.' Although the young boy understood the figurative allusion, the parish priest did not dissuade him.

Angelo spoke also with his uncle Zaverio, expressing his desire to be a priest. Zaverio realised that should Angelo proceed to pursue his vocation he would need fluent Latin. Ceremonies and the liturgy were entirely conducted in Latin and it was essential for the priest to have an adequate grasp of the ancient language. Moreover, all theological writings and lectures were in Latin. Without a fundamental grasp of the language no candidate was permitted to train for the priesthood.

Zaverio accepted Angelo's request to commence studies for the priesthood. He arranged for the young Angelo to have Latin grinds with Don Pietro Bolis, parish priest of the nearby village of Carvico. The experience was an unhappy one, Roncalli recalling years later that he learned one word of Latin for each box on the ears.

Beginning a Religious Education

The next step came the following year when Angelo was enrolled as a day student in the pre-junior seminary at Celana. He was just nine. The seminary had been founded in the period following the Council of Trent by Charles Borromeo (1538–84), the local bishop, and later a saint. A fervent proponent of the reforms decreed by the Council, Borromeo had an enormous impact on the spiritual life of his diocese and the discipline and learning of the clergy.

To the young Angelo the seminary must have seemed vast. It was built in an 'E' shape, each wing rising four storeys. Upwards of one hundred children were educated within its walls.

During the week Angelo boarded with relatives at the nearby Ca' di Rizzi di Pontida. It was his first time being away from his parents and family although he returned home most weekends. The child was desperately unhappy. The austere regime which prevailed in the school was almost unbearable. Corporal punishment was still widely practiced. Children were deprived of meals for small transgressions. When they misbehaved they were put outside the classroom and excluded from activities with other children until they apologised. In addition, he did not get on with his relatives at Ca' di Rizzi.

While visiting the family at Ca' do Rizzi Zaverio found his godson in a miserable state. The child begged his uncle to take him home. Zaverio agreed to speak to Giovanni and Marianna. In addition the relatives demanded more money for Angelo's food and lodging.

In the late Spring of 1892, Roncalli's parents removed him from the school. His hopes of entering the Junior Seminary were dim. Having failed to sit the exams at Celana, the superiors at the Junior Seminary were unwilling to accept him. It seemed that Angelo would spend his life working on the family farm with his father and other siblings.

The young child pleaded with Don Francesco to help him. Rebuzzini recognised the boy's earnestness. Reluctantly he agreed to assist him with his Latin, a prerequisite for enrollment at the Junior Seminary.

Throughout the summer, the young boy helped his father and uncles gather the crops in the morning while in the afternoons he studied at the parochial house with Don Francesco. Throughout the rest of his life, Roncalli often reminisced fondly about the kindness of his parish priest.

In late July, Angelo sat the entrance exam for the college. Admission was by no means assured. Many poor families sent at least one son to the Junior Seminary in the hopes of getting a free education for their child. The diocesan authorities were agreeable to this custom as a number of young men continued to the Major Seminary and were ordained priests.

In September the college authorities at the Junior Seminary of San Giovanni in Arena confirmed Angelo's acceptance at Bergamo. Although he had not excelled at any subject, his results were sufficient and he was accepted for the seminary.

CHAPTER TWO

THE EARLY YEARS AT THE SEMINARY

Shortly before his eleventh birthday, Angelo Roncalli entered the seminary at Bergamo, of which only the chapel exists today. The very concept of the Junior Seminary for young boys vanished in the years following the Second Vatican Council (1962–5).

The seminary system brought into existence following the Council of Trent was designed to provide education and spiritual formation for future priests. In the wake of the sixteenth-century Reformation, the Catholic bishops acknowledged that lack of education had been partly responsible for the spiritual bankruptcy which had sparked off the Protestant reform. Accordingly, it was judged desirable to begin education as early as possible.

Life at the Junior Seminary was rigid, for the Council of Trent decrees modelled the Junior Seminary on the monastic system adopted by St Benedict in the fifth century. The boys slept in dormitories and their entire existence was supervised by priests and matrons. They rose for Mass and prayers at dawn and attended lessons taught by the priests. Reading, mathematics and writing were the fundamental subjects, with history and geography also added in. Latin was taught as the second language. There was little free time for the boys to be on their own as every moment was regulated. Independent thought was discouraged. Those showing strong signs of individuality were dismissed at the end of the scholastic year.

The day was punctuated by visits to the chapel for various devotions and each afternoon the boys had a spiritual meditation. The rosary was recited once in common although the boys were expected to recite it twice more daily on their own. Prayer books filled with novenas and litanies were available and the youths were expected to say these prayers regularly. Several of the prayers were learned by heart.

Meals, taken in common in the refectory, were held in monastic silence, broken only by the voice of a priest reading from the lives of the saints or other edifying books. Exclusion from meals was a regular punishment for a truant child. Once every two weeks the whole college made a day trip to a nearby church or shrine. Letters to family members were allowed on a monthly basis and were read by the superiors prior to posting. Replies were similarly censored.

In November 1891, the Roncalli family, which by now numbered nine children, moved to a large eighteen room house at La Colombéra, still in the village of Sotto il Monte. The expanding family required more space, as did the more distant relatives. The eventual aim was to buy out the family house from the landlord and to own a homestead.

Angelo returned to his family each Christmas and Easter and spent the summer months at Sotto il Monte. These visits were his only opportunity to retain links to his family during the seminary years. Regulations insisted that the young students wear their black uniform even during vacation.

In the summer of 1895, Angelo concluded the three-year preparation at the Junior Seminary. Although he had not achieved much in his academic evaluation, his final report assured the superiors of the Major Seminary that Angelo Roncalli would make a suitable candidate for the priesthood.

In the autumn of 1895, Angelo entered the Major Seminary. Now aged fourteen, Roncalli was still a child and highly impressionable. The seminary was strict on the pubescent boys and particular friendships were discouraged. Sports were insisted upon regardless of talent and cold showers were a regular part of the week. Letters to and from home were more severely censored.

On the advice of a priest of the college, Angelo began to keep a diary which he continued to write, in one form or another, for the rest of his life. It was a largely repetitive set of entries originally destined only for the writer's eyes. The diary was published posthumously in 1965 in book form as *Journal of a Soul*. Sparse on autobiographical details, it is a valuable insight into the spiritual thought and practice of the era and in particular of Angelo Roncalli. Reviewing the diary, preserved in a series of notebooks spanning almost seventy years, Pope John commented wistfully, 'my soul is in these pages'.

On 24 June 1895 Angelo had received the tonsure, the practice by which clerics shaved a small round patch on the crown of the head. This indicated the dedication of the young men to God's future priestly service. As they received the tonsure, they became clerics and entered on the lower rungs of the ecclesiastical ladder. Henceforth they would be differentiated in the eyes of their families and friends. Writing later in his diary, the pious Angelo noted how seriously he took his role, 'I am never alone, even when I am by myself: God, Mary and my Guardian Angel see me; and I am always a seminarian.'

The youths wore black ankle length coats which also set them apart from other children of their age. The purpose of the seminary was to separate the boys from their families and to impress on them their obligations to God.

In September the student body, along with the teachers, travelled to Milan to participate in the National Eucharistic

Congress. The five-day event was an occasion for Italian Catholics to gather and express their faith. Angelo was fascinated by history and marvelled at the gothic cathedral of Milan, which was commenced in 1386 by Archbishop Antonio da Saluzzo and which had taken nearly six centuries to complete. The young man was enchanted by the Ambrosian liturgy, in particular the Chant, named after the celebrated fourth bishop of the city, St Ambrose.

Angelo and his companions were mesmerised by the pomp and ceremony of the Congress. He heard a sermon given by Giuseppe Sarto, the Patriarch of Venice and the future Pope Pius X.

Angelo's companions recalled him as a quiet, serious young man. He participated in all the events of the college although he had little aptitude for sports. The atmosphere of the college was introverted as newspapers were not allowed and the selection of books available was strictly censored.

The following year Angelo was enrolled as a member of the Secular Franciscans. This required of him a vow to live a simple non-materialistic way of life. It did not interfere with the routine of the seminary. It was a private vow to live detached from worldly goods. It was common for religious and lay faithful to take such secular vows and they observed them for the rest of their lives.

Moving Towards the Priesthood

In July 1898 the scholastic year closed as Angelo and his companions advanced further on the road towards priestly ordination. In the chapel the youths received the minor orders of lector and porter. These minor orders reflected a further mirror of the monastic origins of the seminary system. Although no longer an important part of today's priestly formation, for the students they were indications that they had won the approval of the seminary staff.

During each summer Angelo and his companions were allowed to return home. The family had continued to expand. In addition to his surviving older sisters Teresa and Ancilla, Angelo now had younger siblings, Zaverio, Maria Elisa, Assunta Casilda, Alfredo, Giovanni Francesco, Enrica and Giuseppe Luigi. His brother Domenico Giuseppe had died in infancy in March 1888 and Luigi had died in 1898.

Angelo soon became aware of tensions in the family. Some of his siblings resented both his move away and his increasing sophistication. The lack of warmth was a source of pain for the young Roncalli and the holiday period became increasingly irksome. In particular, he found his mother moody and his father distant. Only Uncle Zaverio could understand him and give him advice.

On 28 August 1898 all the seminarians were summoned by the Bishop of Bergamo to attend Pontifical High Mass in the cathedral. The occasion was to mark the feast of St Alexander, the third-century patron saint of Bergamo. The seventeenth-century cathedral of St Alessandro in Colonna had been built on the spot where Alexander was martyred in AD 303.

On that occasion Cardinal Giuseppe Sarto, Patriarch of Venice, presided and preached. The young Roncalli recalled hearing him in Milan at the Eucharistic Congress of 1895 and dutifully noted in his journal that the Patriarch was evidently a saintly man.

A month later Angelo experienced a personal bereavement. He was at home in Sotto il Monte when Don Francesco Rebuzzini died while preparing to celebrate Mass on the morning of 25 September. Angelo recorded the shock of witnessing the sudden death of his mentor; he was just sixteen and highly impressionable. Rebuzzini had been the parish priest of Sotto il Monte for twenty-six years and had known all the families of the district well. In particular he had been a focal point for many families that had migrated from the area due to poverty. He was deeply mourned by the villagers.

On 3 November 1898, the Feast of St Charles Borromeo, Angelo returned to Bergamo and began the new academic year. Studies were centred on theology. As a senior student he was permitted to make excursions around the town of Bergamo but only in the company of another seminarian. The ancient medieval town and in particular the churches and oratories which dotted the streets were a constant source of fascination for him. When allowed out he always searched for a companion who would enjoy visiting the shrines and oratories.

On 25 June 1899 the class concluded the year as the penultimate orders of exorcist and acolyte were conferred. A feast in the refectory followed the ceremony. As usual, only the seminary staff and students attended without any family. Angelo returned home to Sotto il Monte shortly afterwards. Once more he hinted in his diary of tensions between him and some members of his family.

As priestly ordination approached, the seminarians were expected to practice their skills in preaching. On 21 May 1899 Angelo preached his first sermon in public. He had a high-pitched, lilting voice in his native dialect. It was a typical sermon of the era, the reflection of several years of pious formation. Some years later he found the text of the sermon and felt embarrassment at its naivety.

A chance meeting on 17 September 1899 marked a turning point in Angelo's life. While visiting the nearby parish of Ghiaie di Bonate Sopra, Angelo called to see the parish priest, Don Alessandro Locatelli. While the two were talking, Monsignor Giacomo Radini-Tedeschi called to see his old classmate. Locatelli introduced Angelo to the prelate who was working in Rome with the Opera dei Congressi and was a member of the Chapter of St Peter's Basilica at the Vatican. The Opera dei Congressi was a conglomeration of various lay movements in the Church. Radini-Tedeschi was impressed by Angelo's enthusiasm and geniality while the young Angelo was taken by Radini-Tedeschi's earnestness and zeal.

Exactly one year later, Angelo Roncalli met Radini-Tedeschi again. He had been invited by the local curate at Sotto il Monte, Don Ignazio Valsecchi, to take the train to Rome and spend a few days in the Eternal City. Don Ignazio advised Roncalli to call to Santa Marta, the residence of the canons of St Peter's Basilica. Roncalli and Radini-Tedeschi renewed their acquaintance. It was an important meeting, for it introduced Angelo to the practice of introductions and recommendations by which many clerics entered the service of the Holy See.

For the young Roncalli, the short visit to Rome made an indelible impression. Although the time in Rome was short the pilgrims from Sotto il Monte saw a great deal of the city by foot. In St Peter's Basilica they caught a glimpse of the ninety-year-old Pope Leo XIII.

The return journey took Angelo and Don Ignazio to Assisi and Loreto. St Francis lived and died in the Umbrian town of Assisi while the eastern coastal town of Loreto boasted the house where Mary had lived in Palestine, believed to have been transported to Italy in medieval times.

Returning home for a few days before the seminary term began Angelo was surprised when his name was enrolled for a scholarship to study in Rome. Each year the bishop of Bergamo granted a bursary to a number of students to honour the seventeenth-century benefactor Flaminio Cerasola. Accommodation was arranged at the Roman

Seminary close to Piazza Navona. After the first term Angelo returned home for Christmas and prepared for his Roman sojourn.

Chapter Three

Rome, Ordination and the Early Years of Priesthood

Three seminarians from Bergamo arrived in Rome in the early hours of 4 January 1901. Angelo and his two companions were lodged in the large palazzo which housed the Roman seminary at the Piazza San Apollinare, overlooking Piazza Navona.

On his first Sunday in Rome, Angelo made his way to St Peter's Basilica. In a letter home to his parents, he proudly related how Pope Leo XIII had personally blessed him. Although he did not furnish details of the encounter Angelo assured his family that during his brief meeting with the pontiff he thought of his parents and extended family in Sotto il Monte.

Now aged nineteen Angelo could not contain his excitement at obtaining the chance to study in Rome. He had proved himself intellectually capable and his reports in the seminary at Bergamo acknowledged that he had a good memory and a talent for synopsis. Angelo himself underestimated his talent but he tried to work hard. Lectures took place in the adjacent building which was reached by traversing a raised archway.

Although he had evidently enjoyed his time in Bergamo, Angelo waded into Roman life with zest. In Rome he was allowed to attend the theatre and the concert hall, activities prohibited in Bergamo.

Angelo was fascinated by the variety of life in Rome and was amused to hear fellow seminarians from all over Italy chatting in their native dialects. The universality of the city impressed him. He had never seen an Asian or an African before. Seminarians came from all parts of the globe to study in Rome.

Angelo recorded in his notebook a visit to the College of Propaganda Fidei, where seminarians from the mission territories studied. He noted with surprise the colour of their skin, their wide or slanted eyes and their strange languages. He recounted, perhaps not accurately, hearing forty different tongues.

Life was divided between the seminary and lectures in the Pontifical University. During a retreat on 28 April 1901, he recorded in his journal: 'Here in Rome I can say I have all I need. Indeed, there are also opportunities for the acceptance of certain rebuffs to my pride and for the practice of certain mortifications.'

The first scholastic year ended well for Roncalli, who successfully concluded his exams on 25 June. In early July he set off to spend the summer with his family at home.

During the summer a government summons arrived for military service. Like all young men of his age, Roncalli was expected to serve two years in the army. He had hoped to escape the summons and reluctantly entered the Umberto I barracks in Bergamo on 30 November 1901.

While used to the rigours of the seminary, the young Private found the army entirely disagreeable. His companions were pleasant but the regime was rough. The infantry regiment of which he was a member took part in horse riding and manoeuvres in the country outside the city. Despite a strict timetable Angelo was able to visit his family and renew contact with his friends each week.

Military service was reduced from two years to one by a payment from the diocese. On discharge Angelo held the rank of sergeant. Contemporary photographs show the young soldier sporting a large moustache.

Angelo noted in his journal that he saw little to redeem the forced service in barracks. However, it was his first introduction to the raw life of his contemporaries. Tales of sexual exploits evidently appalled him. A year later he wrote of his happiness to be out of the cesspit and back in the seminary.

Angelo returned to Rome in early January 1903 to continue his training. The year in the barracks he summed up as 'the Babylonian captivity'. However, the experience served to broaden his horizons which had been narrowed by the seminary training that he had begun at the age of nine.

Papal Background

On 20 February 1903 Pope Leo XIII celebrated the twenty-fifth anniversary of his pontificate with a year marked by an extraordinary outpouring of affection for the ninety-three-year-old pontiff. Pilgrims came from all over the world to pay homage to the pope. French Catholics who had experienced turbulence in recent decades were among the most fervent and numerous pilgrims.

In the fourth century, the emperor Constantine embraced Christianity and endowed the papacy with lands and annual tributes. Over a thousand years the territories expanded and revenues multiplied. The territories were known colloquially as the Papal States. Since the fall of the Roman Empire in the West in 476, the Italian peninsula was largely made up of small republics, kingdoms and duchies. The Papal States comprised a swathe of land which ran northeastwards from Rome towards the Adriatic Sea close to the Republic of Venice. The Papal States provided a large part of the annual income for the Holy See. During the Napoleonic invasion of Italy in the late eighteenth century the Papal States were briefly suppressed before their restoration in 1800.

The incursions of the French under Napoleon had stirred up Italian nationalism. The mid-nineteenth century was marked by violent revolutions in various states in an effort to establish a single nation. In particular, rebels resented what they saw as papal rule.

In 1860 the Papal States were caught up in hostilities between Lombardy and the south of the peninsula. With the outbreak of the Franco–Prussian war in 1870, Napoleon III withdrew his troops from Rome. King Victor Emmanuel II offered Pope Pius IX his protection. The pope indignantly refused the King's offer.

In September the royal troops entered the Papal States, intent on taking Rome. Pope Pius ordered his small army to make a token defense. On the morning of 20 September the troops entered the city through the Porta Pia. The pope ordered that no resistance be offered and retreated from his residence on the Quirinal Hill to the sixteenth-century Apostolic Palace at the Vatican. The First Vatican Council was in session. Realising the deteriorating political situation the bishops began to leave the city and the pope adjourned the council on 20 October. Until his death eight years later, Pius referred to himself as the 'prisoner of the Vatican'.

The election of the aristocratic Gioachino Pecci as Pope Leo XIII saw a growing sympathy for the figure of the pope. His pragmatic approach to the changing situation both in Italian and global politics was in contrast to Pius' obstinate refusal to countenance the new Italy.

At the end of April 1903, King Edward VII of England visited Rome. The monarch was received by Pope Leo at the Vatican. On 2 May, Kaiser Wilhelm II of Germany was also received at the Vatican by Pope Leo. Angelo noted the visits of these 'heretical' monarchs and took pride in the fact that the pope had received them. Like many of his contemporaries, Angelo believed that the only way towards true ecumenism was for the Protestants to return to the Catholic fold.

Within a few months of the royal visits Pope Leo was dead. When the obsequies were over, the sixty-three cardinal electors gathered in conclave in the Sistine Chapel. On the sixth ballot Giuseppe Sarto, the Patriarch of Venice, was elected Pius X. The choice of name indicated that the benign attitude of Leo was no longer in favour. The uncompromising iron of Pius IX was needed. Sarto was determined to ensure that his pontificate restored the glory some thought Leo had lost.

Angelo joined the crowds in St Peter's Basilica to witness the election. Shortly after the conclave ended Pope Pius appeared at the Hall of Benedictions which overlooked the interior of the basilica while refusing to bless the crowds outside. He later explained that he could not bring himself to look at Rome which had been snatched from the papacy by the Italian government three decades earlier.

In December that year Angelo was ordained with his classmates to the diaconate. This was a transition period of less than a year leading up to his priestly ordination. The final year was filled with lectures and exams which concluded at the end of June.

Ordination to the Priesthood

Following a week-long retreat with the Passionist Fathers on the Caelian Hill, Angelo, along with other deacons, was ordained a priest on 10 August 1904 at the Church of Santa Maria in Monte Santo. The early morning ceremony, which began at 8.30, was officiated by the titular Patriarch of Constantinople and Vice-regent of Rome, Bishop Giuseppe Ceppetelli. None of his family were able to attend the ceremony as the train tickets were too expensive and the price of lodgings was prohibitive.

After the ordination ceremony Angelo walked back across the city to the seminary on his own. The building was deserted as all the seminarians were on their annual vacation at the country villa outside Rome. In the afternoon, the newly-ordained Don Angelo visited several churches on foot. In a letter that evening to his parents and family he assured them that he had prayed for them and looked forward to seeing them for the Feast of the Assumption less than a week later.

The next morning Don Angelo celebrated Mass in the crypt of St Peter's Basilica. Later that day, Pope Pius received some of the newly-ordained priests in a private audience. Angelo told the pope that he came from the north of Italy not far from where Sarto himself was born. The pope offered words of encouragement and a greeting to the Roncalli family asking when he would return to Sotto il Monte. When the young priest said he would be home in a few days the pope sent his blessing to his parents.

Four days later Angelo was greeted by his family when he arrived home. On 15 August, the Feast of the Assumption of the Blessed Virgin Mary, Don Angelo offered Mass for his family and friends in the local parish church. The festivities lasted some two weeks but by September he was back in the seminary in preparation for a license in Canon Law. His studies were abruptly cut short when Canon Radini-Tedeschi was appointed bishop of Bergamo in January 1905.

The new bishop recalled his two meetings with Roncalli and the young man's geniality. Although it meant interrupting his studies, Radini-Tedeschi appointed Angelo as his private secretary. Angelo returned to Bergamo and was present when the new bishop took possession of his cathedral on 9 April 1905.

Life with Radini-Tedeschi

From the start, Angelo was impressed by Radini-Tedeschi's administrative skills. He remained in his diocese, refusing invitations to address congresses and conventions. There were 352 parishes in the diocese with a population of some half million. The bishop set about a systematic visitation of the parishes, each of which lasted two or three days. The pastoral visits, often made on mule or on horseback, gave the bishop a chance to become acquainted with the clergy and people in rural and urban parishes.

From these visits the bishop learned of the problems the people faced. He was aware of the hardships endured by so many and in particular their financial difficulties. For Radini-Tedeschi, one way of alleviating the problems was through a parish-based society called Catholic Action. He supported branches throughout the diocese which promoted social reforms as well as offering practical charitable help.

By now Don Angelo had developed a particular interest in the history of the diocese of Bergamo. While waiting for the bishop to emerge from a meeting, Don Angelo chanced upon an archival account of the pastoral visits of St Charles

Borromeo. In discussion with his bishop, Roncalli proposed publishing the thirty-nine volumes. He received permission to work on the project which became a passion and was to occupy his free time for another fifty years.

In 1907 Don Angelo added another task to his duties. The bishop needed a lecturer on Church history in the diocesan seminary. Although Roncalli did not possess the full teaching qualifications, Radini-Tedeschi appointed his secretary as professor at the seminary at Bergamo.

Throughout the summer Angelo compiled a course on Church history, reading voraciously and making notes. He approached the challenge with quiet discipline and by November he was ready to start lecturing his charges who were only a few years his junior.

Meanwhile Pope Pius X engaged in an examination of the seminaries to ensure that lecturers were teaching sound doctrine. He feared a new brand of heresy called 'Modernism', a secular ideal which he perceived as an interference to traditional Catholic doctrine.

Although Pius' fears were largely exaggerated, on 8 September 1907 he issued the encyclical *Pascendi Dominici Gregis* to combat the errors. The encyclical suppressed the progress of theological development in Catholic universities and seminaries during and after his pontificate. Moreover each diocese was required to establish a committee to oversee the preaching of parish and religious clergy. Although designed to protect Catholic doctrine such commissions alarmed preachers and seminary staff.

Even though the young Roncalli did not teach theology he was careful to avoid any suspicion of heresy. Already theologians and seminary lecturers were being reported to the Holy Office, the department at the Vatican which oversaw theological issues and disputes. In November the Holy Office issued a *monitum*, a warning that those who opposed the wisdom of Pius' encyclical would face automatic excommunication.

Not all were agreed on the danger of Modernism. Cardinal Mariano Rampolla, who had almost been elected to the Papacy in place of Giuseppe Sarto, thought the pope's attitude exaggerated, although he prudently kept his opinions to himself. In an era when the papal office resembled an infallible autocratic monarchy, such views were dangerous.

Don Angelo's main task remained as secretary to the bishop. He was called the 'bishop's shadow' by his fellow clergy not so much for his proximity to Radini-Tedeschi but for his dedication.

The bishop continued to support his people at the time of public strikes for better working conditions. In May 1891 Leo XIII had published an important encyclical, *Rerum Novarum*, which had promoted and defended the basic rights of workers. Radini-Tedeschi was sympathetic to and inspired by Leo's teaching and put it into practice in Bergamo.

On 4 October 1909, eight hundred labourers at a ceramic factory in Ranica, just outside Bergamo, went on strike. They worked ten and a half hours a day for a six-day week. Conditions in the factory were austere. The bishop took the part of the workers and stood by them as negotiations led to a more just outcome for those on strike. Pius did not approve of the participation of bishops in public demonstrations.

The following year the bishop convened a diocesan synod, the first since 1724. It provided the opportunity for a proper census of the diocese and was a summary of Radini-Tedeschi's work to date.

Some months later the Holy Office issued an anti-Modernist oath which was applicable in particular to clergy in teaching positions. It was an attempt to thwart young clergy from espousing such radical thought contrary to Pius' magisterium. The hunt for Modernists continued with increased vigour.

In 1912 Angelo received news of the death of his eighty-eight-year-old uncle, Zaverio. Preaching at his Requiem Mass at Sotto il Monte, Roncalli paid tribute to the pivotal role Zaverio had played within the Roncalli family.

Angelo continued to divide his life between daily service of the bishop and weekly lectures at the seminary. In his spare time he read and edited the archives of St Charles Borromeo which he had located some years earlier in the diocesan library. It was a busy but tranquil life, which changed abruptly in the summer of 1914.

Chapter Four

The Great War, its Aftermath and Propaganda Fidei

On 20 August 1914, Pope Pius X died at the age of seventy-nine. Less than a month earlier the First World War had broken out. Contemporaries reported that the pope had died of a broken heart, but Pius was already in poor health by the early summer.

The pope's death concluded a dramatic decade and a half. Don Angelo would have joined the public mourning but he was at the deathbed of Bishop Radini-Tedeschi who died two days later.

Angelo was desolate. He had grown to love Radini Tedeschi, whom he would ever refer to as 'my Bishop'. Radini-Tedeschi had been fond of Angelo and the two had developed a mutual appreciation. As the bishop's obsequies took place in the cathedral the world's attention focused on Rome and the attendant conclave.

While Pius had been largely liked by the majority of Catholics, the cardinal electors were aware of the bruising effects of the anti-Modernist hunt which had dominated most of his pontificate. The electors were mainly European and realised the importance of having a strong pontificate as the hostilities gained momentum. It was presumed that the next pope would be Italian.

In the event, the Archbishop of Bologna, Cardinal Giacomo della Chiesa gained the required two-thirds majority of thirty-eight votes and emerged as Benedict XV. He had been a cardinal for only three months. A trained diplomat, Della Chiesa had worked in the Vatican Curia. His period in the Secretariat of State had given him first-hand knowledge of the workings of the central government of the Church. As Benedict XV, he tried to convince the belligerents to sue for peace. His efforts to keep Italy neutral failed when war was declared on the Austro–Hungarian empire.

Angelo, no longer the bishop's secretary, had divided his time between lecturing at the seminary and organising adult education lectures on historical and cultural affairs. In May 1915 he was conscripted to the Italian army, shortly followed by his brother Zaverio and later Giuseppe.

As a priest, Angelo was billeted at the hospital in Bergamo. Life, already difficult for the poor of the district, became even more challenging. Rations were introduced and wages fell. The ever-present fear that battle would come to Italy created an atmosphere of uncertainty. Each day newspapers carried detailed accounts of battles and a list of the dead. Angelo ministered to those brought from the battlefields to recuperate in the military hospital of Bergamo. While he despised the war he admired the soldiers whom he met and tended to in the wards. In his free time he visited his family at Sotto il Monte and composed a commemorative book in tribute to Radini-Tedeschi entitled 'My Bishop'.

The war dragged on until an armistice was finally signed on 11 November 1918. By that stage around sixteen million civilians and soldiers had been killed across the European continent. The war was followed by an influenza pandemic which claimed a further twenty to fifty million lives around the globe.

Even before the war ended Angelo had noted in a letter to a friend that there were hardly any casualties in his hospital. The epicentre of the war had moved to France and people were beginning to adjust to imminent peace.

The Aftermath of the Great War

In February 1918 Don Angelo was appointed dean of a newly-founded student residence in Bergamo. While he continued to attend to his soldiers he now turned his energies to opening a student hostel. Demobbed from the army, he undertook the care of students while they attended the nearby university. The war had decimated the male population and for the first time women were taking their place in the world of academia.

As a father figure Don Angelo was popular among the students. The war had taught him the frailty of humans. No longer was he shocked by the barracks humour he had heard during his military service. He understood the pressure soldiers experience in a challenging profession.

On a personal level Angelo had the satisfaction of seeing his family finally purchase the homestead of La Colombéra, which had been the family home since 1891. Correspondence shows the growing distance between himself and his moody mother and taciturn father. He made attempts to cheer them up in difficult circumstances and on several occasions contributed financially to the family.

There was a spirit of optimism in the air. Italy had emerged from the war on the winning side. The country needed stability and to build itself up following the four years of hostilities. The Italians embraced the fragile peace which had been won at so great a cost.

In addition to his duties at the student residence, Don Angelo became chaplain to the Catholic Women's Union. With so many young widows, the union became a focal point for a number of women of the city. As with the students, Angelo's kindly nature drew people to him. He noted his concern in his diary resolving never to make people depend on him.

In late October 1919 Don Angelo travelled to Rome to participate in a conference on the Catholic Women's Union. He composed a memo which he wished to present to Pope

Benedict XV to explain the initiative and to seek papal approval.

Post-war Europe was vastly different from the years before the hostilities had claimed the lives of millions of military personnel. Women now came to occupy situations previously filled only by men. The Church had new opportunities and obligations in this regard.

The political scene had changed dramatically in the aftermath of the war. A Sicilian priest, Don Luigi Sturzo (1871–1959), had founded the *Partito Popolare Italiano* (Italian People's Party), which embraced Catholic values. Roncalli liked the party with its overtly Christian sentiment, which contrasted with the nationalism proposed by the Fascists.

When the conference ended, Roncalli remained in Rome until he was summoned to an audience with Pope Benedict. Roncalli had requested the audience through Canon Pietro Morlani, the brother of his family's former landlord. The pontiff had been a personal friend of Radini-Tedeschi and had read a copy of Roncalli's biography. He listened with interest to the young priest's account of the newly-formed association, expressing concern over the workers' conditions in Bergamo. A native of Genoa and later bishop of the city, Benedict was relatively familiar with the issues facing people of the region.

Returning to provincial Bergamo, where post-war changes in Europe and Russia were less obvious, Angelo Roncalli added the spiritual direction of the seminarians to his duties. He soon became popular among his young charges, combining wisdom and common sense. Things were to change the following year when he was summoned to Rome. A new task awaited him.

Working for the Missions

In a letter dated 6 December 1920 Cardinal William van Rossum requested Bishop Marella of Bergamo to release Don Angelo Roncalli to work at the Congregation for the Propagation of the Faith. The office, colloquially known as Propaganda Fidei, had been founded in the seventeenth century during a flurry of global missionary activity following the discovery of new territories by European explorers. A pontifical university, the Urbanianum, trained students from all over the world.

With improved methods of transport in the nineteenth and twentieth centuries, missionary work rapidly expanded. Funds were needed to support the work of the various religious congregations and priests who settled in the missionary territories. Italy was a natural source for funds. The genial Angelo was judged the most suitable person to work in the field of fundraising throughout the country.

Angelo was dismayed by the summons, protesting to the bishop that he was not equipped with the necessary skills. However, his years as secretary to Radini-Tedeschi had honed his abilities. His protests were unheeded and van Rossum confirmed the appointment in early January 1921. Don Angelo travelled to Rome in mid-January for his interview with the Prefect. The cardinal encouraged the thirty-nine-year-old priest to dedicate his energies to the Missions. He was given an office in the large building overlooking the Column of the Immaculate Conception close to the Spanish Steps, where he began work on 18 January. During the month of April Roncalli visited several Italian dioceses to fundraise for the missions.

Pope Benedict had written an encyclical, *Maximum Illud*, on 30 November 1919 dedicated to the missions. This was an era of extraordinary triumphalism but skill and dedication were required to ensure the lasting success of Christianity in the new territories. Benedict also urged the mission fields to provide their own indigenous clergy and hierarchies, an enterprise which he acknowledged would need time and patience. Part of the funding for the training of indigenous clergy was to come from the traditionally Catholic countries of Europe.

On a domestic note, Don Angelo was assigned a large modern apartment in a newly-built palazzo on the Via Volturno close by the railway station. Although his days were spent at the office he invited his sisters Ancilla and Maria to come to live with him. In return, they took care of the house. He later invited his former rector at the Roman seminary, Monsignor Vincenzo Bugarini, to take lodgings at his apartment.

Angelo had little experience as a fundraiser. The cardinal dispatched him almost immediately to visit France and Germany to see how local groups funded missionary work. Leaving Rome by train on 17 December, Angelo visited Munich, Cologne and Brussels. This was his first foray outside Italy.

Roncalli's friendly manner made it easy to forge relationships. He only spoke Italian, although he succeeded in communicating with many of the German ecclesiastics in Latin.

Three weeks after his return to Rome in early January 1922 Pope Benedict XV died. The pontiff had caught a chill while waiting in a cold corridor while a footman searched for a key to the papal apartments. The chill soon turned to fatal pneumonia. For the second time, Don Angelo was able to witness a papal funeral and preparations for a conclave.

As with most conclaves, the College of Cardinals was divided between a handful of realistic candidates. Cardinal Merry del Val had been Secretary of State to Pius X and Pietro Gasparri had occupied the same position under Benedict XV. Supporters of each candidate were unable to secure the required thirty-six votes. A compromise came in the shape of Achille Ratti, whom Benedict had appointed Archbishop of Milan five months previously.

Ratti appeared an unusual choice. For almost two decades he had worked at the celebrated Ambrosian Library prior to his appointment as Prefect of the Vatican Library in 1914. Pope Benedict XV requested him to leave his post in 1918 and take up a position as Apostolic Visitor, or papal representative, to Poland. The aftermath of the war had required Church authorities to act rapidly in securing a place in the public forum.

The following spring Ratti's rank was raised to Apostolic Nuncio, ambassador of the Holy See to Warsaw. Ratti faced a difficult situation in Poland. Not trained in the diplomatic service, he was caught in the crossfire of conflicting political and religious differences, notably between Poland and Silesia. He found it difficult to pick his way through the diplomatic minefield.

In early 1921 Ratti was recalled from Poland. On 3 June he was made a cardinal and appointed Archbishop of Milan. It was a promotion of sorts. Benedict had been obliged to replace Ratti with a more experienced diplomat in Poland. Milan was seen as a reward for his distinguished scholarly service and his efforts in Poland.

Ratti was acknowledged as a pragmatist. It was difficult to label him as either a liberal or a conservative. As the world tried to cement the peace initiatives of the armistice Ratti seemed a good choice. For five days, the fifty-three cardinals cast their votes unsuccessfully. On the fourteenth ballot, Ratti was elected pope.

Angelo Roncalli was pleased with the election of the Archbishop of Milan. Angelo's interests in the life and times of St Charles Borromeo corresponded with Ratti's. Pius' election did not impinge on Roncalli, who undertook a series of journeys around Italy to drum up spiritual and financial support for the missions. Writing home to his family, he shared his enthusiasm and remarked on the regional differences between the different parts of the country. The journeys to the north renewed his acquaintances with bishops who had known Radini-Tedeschi. Committees were established to assist the missions. His trip to Sicily in May 1924 intrigued him. The island was steeped in history and artistic treasures. In particular he praised the food of the region.

Roncalli had the satisfaction of seeing the fruits of his work pay off. Several dioceses and parishes set up committees to support the missions by prayer and practical support. The financial ledgers recorded increasing income for the new mission territories. Angelo's genial character and organisational abilities were bearing fruit, although he had his first taste of bureaucracy as he tried to inspire some of his staff to work to the best of their ability.

Don Angelo made the most of his time in Rome, becoming better-acquainted with its myriad of churches and historic monuments. In his free time he worked on the project of editing the Acts and Life of St Charles Borromeo. The office continued to grow. Although the fundraising office principally served to build infrastructures and provide scholarships for clergy, there was also an important humanitarian aspect. Where a country or territory experienced physical hardships, Roncalli tried to make funds available. Hospitals and medical needs were funded throughout the missionary lands, which largely corresponded to the developing world. Roncalli also became a popular guest speaker at confraternity meetings and novenas.

By now Roncalli was fully immersed in the Roman way of life. He was happy in the city. He had moved to a larger residence with his sisters and his former rector at the church of Santa Maria in Via Lala. Monsignor Bugarini died in the house on 14 February 1924. Nine months later Roncalli added a new duty to his workload when he was appointed Professor of Patristics at the Lateran University. It seemed that he was destined to live the rest of his life in Rome.

Chapter Five

Archbishop and Life in the East

On 17 February 1925, Angelo Roncalli was summoned to the Apostolic Palace at the Vatican to see Cardinal Pietro Gasparri, the Secretary of State. Although used to meeting various curial officials, an audience with the Cardinal Secretary of State was unusual. Roncalli entered the Palace at the Bronze Door to the side of Bernini's colonnade at St Peter's Square. Saluted by the Swiss Guard who attended the entrance, Roncalli ascended the marble flight of stairs leading to the Courtyard of St Damasus. He crossed the square and was admitted to the Secretariate on the third floor of the sixteenth-century Apostolic Palace, then ushered into the cardinal's presence.

Roncalli had received no agenda and was apprehensive about what lay in store. After short formalities the cardinal explained the reason for the audience: the Church in Bulgaria was experiencing severe difficulties. It was, in the cardinal's very words, 'in a mess'. Catholics, Orthodox Christians and Muslims seemed to be at each other's throats. The pope wanted somebody to go and sort out the difficult situation and Pius had personally chosen Roncalli.

Four days later the pope received Monsignor Roncalli in a private audience. The pope explained his thinking. Bulgaria did not have full diplomatic relations with the Holy See. Accordingly Pius did not wish to send a high-ranking prelate.

'Your name was suggested to me for this visitation', the pope explained, 'and I was very happy about it. I was told that your title of monsignor would be enough but I replied: "It is not a good thing when an apostolic prelate goes to a country and has to deal with the bishops without being one himself. So I decided you should be consecrated Archbishop".'

That evening Angelo recorded in his diary an account of the unexpected meeting with the pope. The new task was completely unforseen. He was given less than a month to prepare for his episcopal consecration and for his departure for Bulgaria. On 19 March Roncalli was consecrated in the Church of San Carlo on Rome's Via del Corso. The consecrator was Cardinal Giovanni Tacci, Prefect for the Oriental Churches.

The splendid church, dear to the clergy of Milan and its environs, dwarfed Roncalli's family and friends who gathered for the ceremony. Angelo's mother and father sat with their family in the front rows and watched the elaborate ritual unfold.

After a few days of festivities – which also included a private audience for the family with Pope Pius – it was time for Roncalli to turn his mind to his new mission.

While everyone congratulated the new papal representative, Roncalli was left to work out what his new engagement would mean in practice. The cardinal secretary had told him of the close links between Italy and Bulgaria and that he should pay special attention to the royal Bulgarian court.

The new archbishop had domestic matters to deal with on his return to Sotto il Monte. With his departure for Sofia, the capital of Bulgaria, he had been obliged to give up his apartment in Rome. It was unthinkable for his sisters to accompany him to Bulgaria. With a higher stipend, Roncalli was able to rent a portion of an old Roncalli property at Sotto il Monte. His sisters took up residence there with the pretence that they would keep the house for their brother when he took his vacation. From that year until his election as pope in 1958, Angelo spent two holiday periods most years with his sisters, the closest of all his siblings.

Life in Bulgaria

On 23 April 1925, Archbishop Roncalli boarded the Orient Express in Milan which would sweep him to a new life in the East. In the trunks which accompanied the diplomat were several books including his *Acts of St Charles* and Pastor's *The History of the Popes*. Also included were the first volumes of Jacques-Paul Migne's collection of the writings of the Greek and Latin Fathers of the Church. Over the following three decades Roncalli bought three hundred volumes which he eventually left in his will to the seminary at Bergamo. He also took with him a dinner service given by the clergy of Bergamo and linen provided by his family. A separate trunk contained his ecclesiastical garments.

Bulgaria at the time was in political turmoil. It had been punished following World War I by having its territories reduced. The war itself failed to unite the populace and allowed centuries-old suspicions and rivalries to emerge. In 1054 Latin Catholics and Orthodox Christians had excommunicated each other following a schism at Constantinople. The Bulgarian Church had broken from union with the Patriarch of Constantinople in 1872.

The new papal representative, now aged forty-four, arrived in Sofia after a journey of two days. He was greeted at the station by the Capuchin Bishop Vinkenti Peev and accompanied to his modest lodgings at Liuline Steet. Just days earlier a Catholic church had been set on fire in the city and tensions were running high. The collapse of the Ottoman empire, the emergence of Arab nationalism and the Russian revolution had destabilised the area. Sofia had become the capital when the Kingdom of Bulgaria was established in 1908. He immediately made contact with the clergy and people of his new flock. The winter snows prohibited his movement outside the city.

Roncalli set about learning Bulgarian, which he found extremely difficult. He lamented that he had not studied languages like his fellow diplomats. Latin was of little use to him on the ground dealing with the Bulgarians. Each day he spent a couple of hours learning and practicing the language but made slow progress.

Some sixty thousand Catholics were spread throughout the country whose overall population numbered some six million. A portion of the Catholic population lived in cities while the rest were scattered throughout rural Bulgaria. There were also a number of Catholics of Macedonian origin who had settled in the country.

For the first time Angelo Roncalli found himself living in a country where Catholics were in a minority. Pope Pius had told him to intervene with the squabbling Christians and protect the Church from Muslim influence. His task was to be a pacifier. Even with his serene personality it was a daunting task. On 26 August Archbishop Roncalli visited the Orthodox Holy Synod in Sofia.

The vast majority of Christians were Orthodox. Ecumenism was a concept in its infancy. Catholics viewed the Orthodox as heretics while Orthodox viewed Catholics as proselytisers. For most Catholics, ecumenism consisted mainly of prayer for the return of heretics and schismatics to the One True Church. There was little understanding for the shared origins of the faith and often less respect.

Roncalli's reading, especially of the Greek Fathers, however, equipped him well in his dialogue with the Orthodox, who had rarely heard Catholic bishops quote from their Eastern patristic patrimony.

The Orthodox Church viewed Rome with suspicion. The new nuncio, despite his affability, represented a foreign ecclesiastical power. This was made more complex as Roncalli was Italian. The papal representative had no formal training in diplomacy, not having attended the Pontifical Academy for Ecclesiastics, the prestigious school for papal diplomats in Rome. The Bulgarian language continued to be a stumbling block.

Archbishop Roncalli tried to encourage the Uniate Catholics whose churches were in union with Rome. He was astonished at the poor levels of education among both clergy and bishops. His lodgings were unsuitable for him to host functions. In his letters home to family and friends he confessed that he found his experience lonely.

When Cardinal Gasparri first gave him the news of his transfer to Bulgaria he had hinted that this was an entrance to the diplomatic service. After a short posting he would most likely be sent to Argentina, a flourishing country in Latin America. The nunciature was based in Buenos Aires which possessed a large migrant Italian population.

As the years passed Angelo found it difficult to make substantial headway. There were severe tensions and jealousies among the Uniate clergy and efforts at friendship were seldom reciprocated. Even missives from his superiors at the Congregation for Oriental Churches failed to cheer him up. This was a long-term project for the Holy See, and it required tact and patience in equal measure. He was nostalgic for home and news from his friends. His annual trips to Rome to report to his superiors heightened his sense of isolation.

As the years passed without promotion to a higher mission, Roncalli's friends in Rome commiserated on the neglect. He took little comfort and threw himself more heartily into his work.

In the Roman scheme of things, it is considered something of a failure for a non-diplomat to leave the Roman Curia. Following the death of Cardinal Eugenio Tosi on 7 January 1929, rumours circulated that Roncalli might succeed him as Archbishop of Milan. Roncalli heard the gossip although he dismissed it as such in a letter to his sisters Ancilla and Maria.

At the same time, the Roman Question was finally resolved. On 11 February 1929 King Victor Emmanuel III and Pope Pius XI agreed a treaty resolving the bitter quarrel between the Holy See and the Italian authorities which had lasted almost seventy years. In ceding the Papal States and various possessions the Holy See agreed to recognise the Italian State. The pact was signed by Benito Mussolini and Cardinal Pietro Gasparri. The Holy See established a 108-acre city state at the Vatican and was allowed retain a number of extraterritorial possessions, notably churches and basilicas in Rome. In addition, approximate financial restitution was awarded from the Italian government for the lands and properties of the confiscated Papal States. The Holy See was granted independence from Italy although its geographical situation at the heart of Rome ensured its continued immersion in the Italian *modus vivendi.* The Lateran Treaty also ensured the survival of the Vatican diplomatic service, the oldest such network in the world.

While most first diplomatic postings lasted three to five years, Roncalli remained for ten years, until 1935, in Bulgaria. The new Archbishop of Milan had been appointed in August 1929. Once more, it appeared as if Roncalli was forgotten in the East.

The following year, in the autumn of 1930, Roncalli felt the unexpected brunt of Pope Pius' rage when the thirty-five-year-old King Boris III of Bulgaria married Giovanna, the daughter of King Victor Emmanuel III. Roncalli took care of the dispensation for the Orthodox sovereign to marry the Catholic princess and the marriage was celebrated at Assisi on 25 October 1930.

Roncalli attended the splendid nuptials which were celebrated in the thirteenth-century Basilica of St Francis. It was understood that the king would allow his children to be baptised Catholics and that the royal couple would not undertake a second marriage ceremony in the Orthodox tradition.

When the couple travelled to Sofia a week later they took part in a ceremony according to the Orthodox rites. The pope was furious as this was in direct contravention to the law of the Catholic Church and had been a precondition for the princess' dispensation. The following year, notwithstanding the pope's displeasure, Roncalli received the title Apostolic Delegate although he remained in Bulgaria as the pope's personal representative.

When the princess bore a child a year after the marriage the infant was baptised Orthodox. The king argued that as monarch of an Orthodox country, he had done no less than his duty as the male child was heir to the throne. Roncalli was once more called to task by the pontiff who insisted that the child should have been christened in his mother's faith. Pius observed bitterly that King Boris had reneged on his matrimonial promises. Hopes that Bulgaria would thus one day become Catholic were left unrealised.

A welcome change came on 17 November 1934 when a cipher arrived at the Delegation with news of the Archbishop's transfer. Roncalli's hopes of going to Argentina were dashed when he learned that he would be the Apostolic Visitor in nearby Turkey and Greece. It would prove a complex double appointment: Turkey was predominantly Islamic and Greece was Orthodox Christian. Both countries were traditionally hostile to each other. While Turkey moved towards laicisation, Greece remained tenacious to its Christian roots.

The Vatican mission was based in Istanbul, which was still called Constantinople by many Christians, including Roncalli. Angelo consoled himself with the fact that he was well-acquainted with the reality of Orthodox and Muslims living side by side. For that reason his superiors must have wished to appoint him to these countries. The residence would be in the Turkish capital.

Life in Turkey and Greece

Angelo Roncalli set off for Constantinople on 4 January 1935. In the farewells he realised the affection he had won from so many sources, but he could not hide his satisfaction that his exile had come to an end. In bidding farewell to his neighbours for ten years, Roncalli told his listeners that he would always be happy to meet again. He recalled an Irish tradition which he had learned about from his Irish assistant, Monsignor Thomas Ryan. On Christmas Eve a candle is placed in the window of homes throughout the country. It is a signal that if Mary and Joseph were to pass by once more they would find a welcome.

> Wherever I may go, if a Bulgarian passes by my door, whether it's nighttime or whether he's poor, he will find that candle lighted in my window. Knock, Knock. You won't be asked whether you're a Catholic or not.

Roncalli was already familiar with Constantinople, a vastly more interesting city than Sofia. The Ottoman influence was still very much in evidence and he enjoyed exploring the city. The posting was marginally more prestigious. The Roman emperor Septimius Severus had rebuilt the old town of Byzantium in 196, and the Emperor Constantine had dedicated it as his capital and renamed it Constantinopolis in the fourth century. Constantinople was an ancient city built layer upon layer.

As with every city he visited, he enjoyed wandering about and exploring the ancient churches and monuments. Slowly he built up a network of contacts with Muslims and Orthodox Christians. The latter were suspicious that the new nuncio was under instruction to convert the Orthodox to Catholicism. Partly due to the Great War, the number of Orthodox in Turkey was some one hundred thousand, while the population of Catholics was only around thirty-five thousand. In Istanbul, Catholics were less than two hundred. The diplomatic circuit in Sofia had been restricted. Here in Constantinople regular receptions in international embassies introduced him to a wider circle.

Shortly after his arrival, Roncalli began a systematic visitation of Catholics in the country. He found small communities in Cilicia. These mostly comprised the families of foreign business people. In Tarsus, the home of St Paul, there were just twenty Catholic families.

On 28 July 1935 news arrived by phone that Angelo's father had died at the age of eighty-one. Roncalli was not able to return in time for the funeral and sent a long affectionate letter to his mother. In the late summer he returned home to Bergamo to visit his family and comfort his widowed mother. In October Italy invaded Abyssinia in a move by which Italy tried to assert its rights to colonise the area. The war did not concern Angelo directly as he returned to take up his post in Constantinople.

Turkey had become a republic in 1923 under a ruling party led by Mustafa Kemel, who was renamed Kemel Atatürk in 1934. Christianity had dwindled partly because the Turkish authorities saw the faith as foreign. Roncalli made a favourable impact on many Turkish politicians and succeeded in learning elementary Turkish. While his efforts to learn Bulgarian had not been very successful, this time Roncalli was determined to speak in the language of the country. 'If in Rome Christ is a Roman, in Turkey he must be a Turk,' he noted in his diary. Roncalli spent months learning about Islam, the majority faith of the country, although he had almost no interaction with Muslims. His mission was simply to defend and build up the Catholic presence in the country. Efforts to make converts to Christianity was severely prohibited by the government.

On 16 May 1936 the new nuncio authorised the use of some Turkish phrases in the Latin liturgy. At Mass in the Cathedral of the Holy Spirit, the Epistle and Gospel were read in Turkish after their proclamation in Latin. It was a presage of his intentions when calling the Second Vatican Council some three decades later. His efforts earned him a reprimand from the Congregation for the Oriental Churches.

Relations with Greece were more difficult. The monarchy had been restored in 1935 and the largely Orthodox Greek population – some ninety-eight per cent – wished to have little to do with the Catholic Church. The fact that Italy had launched the assault on Abyssinia was a further obstacle for the Italian Angelo Roncalli.

When he presented his credentials to King George, Roncalli was reassured by the monarch that Catholics would be free to practice their religion. The situation changed in the following years as nationalist forces convinced the king that Rome's missionary efforts would destabilise nationalist sentiment.

The Greek political authorities were still trying to organise themselves following the aftermath of the First World War. They were suspicious of the nuncio's true intentions. Roncalli was faced with the challenge of soothing the government, which saw foreigners as political rivals. In August 1938 the Greek monarch, King George, promulgated laws which prevented Catholics from proselytising and placed Catholic schools, hospitals and orphanages under state surveillance. The experience in Greece broadened Roncalli's knowledge of Christianity outside Italian Catholicism. He travelled extensively throughout Greece, visiting Christian shrines and Orthodox monasteries.

As the Second World War drew closer, Roncalli was particularly concerned about the fate of thousands of Jews who were already fleeing persecution in Germany. The new German ambassador to Turkey, Franz von Papen, arrived in Istanbul in August 1939. The ambassador, the former Chancellor, attended Mass regularly at the nunciature. Almost immediately Roncalli asked him for help on behalf of the Jewish refugees. At first the help required was practical: food, clothes, medicine and money. When von Papen hesitated, Roncalli pointed out that the refugees had been displaced by the forces of the Third Reich. The Jews were to be a constant concern for Roncalli. Writing in his diary, Angelo expressed his sadness at their sufferings. 'The poor children of Israel. I hear their groans about me daily. I am distressed and I do my utmost to help them.'

World War II

On 1 September 1939 Germany invaded Poland in the opening act of World War II. Atatürk's death on 10 November 1938 unsettled the political situation in Turkey. Roncalli was on a visit to Greece when he heard of Atatürk's death and returned to Constantinople.

On 10 February 1939 Pope Pius XI died at the Vatican, bringing to an end his seventeen-year pontificate. The death of the eighty-one-year-old pontiff came as no surprise to most. The last years of the pope's life were overshadowed by the threat of war. In March 1937 he had composed two important encyclicals warning against the rise of atheistic Communism and Fascism. According to rumours in Vatican circles the pope was about to deliver a speech the next day condemning the Nazi party.

Some days later a telegram arrived in Istanbul bearing the news that Angelo's mother Marianna had died, on 20 February, of influenza at the age of eighty-five. As with his father's funeral Angelo did not attend. Such were the sacrifices expected in the service of the Holy See. A Mass was celebrated in the cathedral of the city attended by many clerics. Roncalli was deeply touched by the gesture of his fellow clergy.

During the conclave at the beginning of March 1939, the sixty-two cardinal electors realised the need for a politically-adept pope. After the shortest conclave of the century, lasting just two days, their choice fell on the former Secretary of State, Cardinal Eugenio Pacelli. As a mark of respect for his patron Pacelli took the name Pius XII.

Roncalli had known Pacelli for several years and admired his cultural and diplomatic skills. The beginning of the pontificate was overshadowed by the outbreak of hostilities which soon engulfed Europe and beyond.

To celebrate the election, Roncalli was received in audience by the Ecumenical Patriarch of Constantinople,

Benjamin, honorary head of the Eastern Orthodox Ecclesiastically Independent Churches. The papal delegate dressed in his most splendid robes to greet the Patriarch. The two exchanged an embrace and promised to pray for each other. Ostensibly the occasion was to convey the Roman pontiff's greeting. Both men got on well during their brief encounter and a correspondence began between the Vatican embassy and the Patriarchate. It was a small progression in the lengthy process of normalising relations between Constantinople and Rome. Roncalli was pleased also that the Orthodox Patriarch of Athens was represented at Pius' coronation at the Vatican in March.

Italy entered the war in June 1940, becoming an ally of Germany. Roncalli was deeply disturbed by the developing hostilities. Greece had also entered the war, in October 1940. The Congregation for the Oriental Churches advised Roncalli to visit Greece and observe the situation. However, the war made life difficult. Travel was restricted and rations were imposed. For Roncalli the situation was made all the more complex as Italian battalions occupied parts of the country.

Von Papen and Roncalli regularly discussed the developments of the European war. Roncalli reported several summaries of their conversations to his superiors in Rome, adding that he felt von Papen was overly optimistic about Adolf Hitler. His superiors agreed. Turkey was an important listening post where Roncalli sharpened his political skills.

While the German delegation tried to convince Roncalli of the government's aims to end the war, the nuncio was sceptical. His caution proved well-founded when Germany invaded the Soviet Union on 22 June 1941. Hitler was determined to dominate central Europe in an escalating war.

The Holy See continued to receive reports from the diplomatic missions throughout the world and monitored the casualties. As the war progressed in Greece, Roncalli's visits were limited. He insisted on visiting the prisoners of war and tried to offer spiritual and material help. In particular he facilitated the flow of information regarding soldiers. At Pius' instruction the Vatican had established an informal network to help families locate displaced soldiers. Roncalli supplied information which he gleaned from his sources and set up 'The Hearth of Divine Providence', an information centre to help families of prisoners of war. On 15 December Roncalli wrote to the Turkish Christians to help the Greek children orphaned by the war.

In 1943 Roncalli wrote to King Boris recalling his years in Turkey and imploring the King to allow the refugees temporary sanctuary as they fled to Palestine. The following year, when Jews were deported to Hungary, Roncalli enlisted the help of the Swedish diplomat Raoul Wallenberg.

Speaking years later at the cause for the beatification of John XXIII, von Papen recalled his dealings with the papal nuncio. He estimated that Roncalli had intervened to save the lives of some twenty-four thousand Jews, many of whom were children, during the war years.

Chapter Six

Nuncio to France

On 6 December 1944 a telegram arrived with unexpected news. Roncalli's service to Turkey and Greece had been terminated by Pope Pius XII. He was to make a round of farewell visits and take up a new post. Almost three weeks were to pass before it was confirmed that he would be the new papal nuncio to France.

The events leading up to the surprise nomination began in Paris earlier that summer. On 30 June, General Charles de Gaulle was received in private audience by Pope Pius. The pope conveyed his congratulations on the change of government. He spoke of the ongoing feud which was ripping Europe apart, lamenting the actions of the Soviets in Poland and the fate of Eastern Europe.

De Gaulle had to convince the French people of his determination for change. Among the requests was the transfer of the Apostolic Nuncio, Archbishop Valerio Valeri. De Gaulle argued that he had ostensibly supported the Vichy regime led by Marshal Philippe Pétain which had collaborated with the Nazis.

Pius refused to accommodate de Gaulle's request, reminding the French leader that nuncios are appointed to the State rather than the government in power. Assurances were given that Valeri would cooperate with the new authorities. De Gaulle insisted however that a new nuncio should be appointed in recognition of the dramatic change in French political life. The pope steadfastly opposed the

French overtures although he accepted the credentials of de Gaulle's personal envoy to the Holy See, Hubert Guérin.

On 26 August, de Gaulle celebrated the Liberation of Paris by attending a service at Notre Dame cathedral. This sent a signal to the French people of de Gaulle's piety and his agreement with the role the Church played in French society. Despite appeals from influential French Catholics, the pope continued to support Valeri and refused to remove him. The Russian government officially recognised the de Gaulle government and accredited an ambassador to France.

Pius was outraged at the affront. He dispatched Cardinal Eugène Tisserant to France to find out what was going on and to placate de Gaulle. Tisserant was a good choice as he had been a highly decorated military intelligence officer during World War I. In France the Dean of the diplomatic corps had traditionally been the Apostolic Nuncio. It was him who presented New Year's greetings on behalf of the diplomatic corps to the French head of state. Unless the Church acted quickly the new Russian Ambassador would assume the role and deliver the address. Such an action would *ipso facto* tilt the balance of favour away from the Church.

Pius was forced to abandon Valeri and appoint a new ambassador acceptable to the French government. His first choice was Archbishop Giuseppe Fietta who had served as nuncio to Argentina since 1936. Fietta was informed of his appointment on 2 December but citing reasons of health declined the prestigious post. Time was running out as a new ambassador had to be in place and accredited by early January.

Pius acted quickly. He appointed Roncalli to Paris and summoned him to Rome prior to taking up the appointment. Roncalli was mystified by the unexpected change. He knew nothing of Fietta's refusal and duly arrived in Rome to meet with the pontiff.

On 28 December, Roncalli was received in private audience. Pope Pius reassured him of his complete confidence, advising him that the mission to France was not without tensions. Although he did not share the whole story with Roncalli, Pius reassured him that he had personally chosen him for his merits. Roncalli furnished an account of the audience in a letter to his former secretary Giacomo Testa.

That evening Roncalli visited Valeri to hear his side of the story. The ex-nuncio was bruised from his unexpected exit and advised Roncalli to be aware of certain bishops. To assist him, Valeri gave Roncalli copies of previous New Year greetings which might prove useful.

Arrival in Paris

On 29 December 1944 Roncalli flew from Rome's Ciampino military airport to Paris to take up residence at the Apostolic Nunciature at 10 Avenue du Président Wilson. He went directly to make a courtesy call at the Foreign Office and received the archbishop of Paris, Cardinal Suhard, that evening at his new home.

On New Year's Day, the new papal ambassador was received by de Gaulle at the Champs-Élysées and presented his credentials. With this done he could now claim the title of Dean of the Diplomatic Corps and deliver the New Year greetings.

Dressed in a black soutane with a magenta watered-silk cape over his shoulders, Roncalli launched into a formal speech in guttural French. The handful of ambassadors stood stiffly during the address. By lunchtime the Holy See had formally recognised the de Gaulle government. At least superficially, diplomatic goodwill had been restored between the French government and the Holy See, but Europe was still at war. While de Gaulle solidified his position the echoes of war had moved eastwards. There were cautious hopes that the hostilities would soon end.

The deaths of Adolf Hitler and Benito Mussolini in April 1945 signalled the end of the war in Europe. Japan formally surrendered in September 1945, ending the war. The war had claimed the lives of an estimated sixty million. Those who survived bore severe psychological scars which would fade, but never heal. A generation had been seared with the horrors of human hatred.

After the War

De Gaulle was determined to rid France of the traces of the Vichy regime. He demanded that the Holy See remove a number of bishops whom he claimed had 'collaborated' with the regime. This was to be the first test of Roncalli's mettle in France.

Rome was opposed to the bishops' demotion not simply for what could be argued as an unjust punishment. There was also the fear that the new government might try to interfere in the provision of new bishops. In Roncalli's view, what was needed was prevarication.

De Gaulle sensed what the new nuncio was up to and in a conversation in the early summer he advised Roncalli that he would even accept a token number of bishops' retirements. Furthermore, as rumours circulated that Pius intended creating a large number of cardinals at a consistory, de Gaulle argued that the pontiff should honour bishops whom he deemed not to have supported the Vichy government.

Roncalli protested that he had absolutely no power to suggest names to the pope. De Gaulle then produced a list which included the archbishops of Rouen, Rennes and Toulouse and requested that he forward them to the relevant powers in Rome. Reluctantly Roncalli did so, although he accompanied the recommendations with a note explaining why two of the three in his opinion were not particularly suitable. Pius considered the French president's suggestions and to Roncalli's surprise all three were named among thirty-two new cardinals created at the Vatican on 18 February 1996.

As nuncio, Roncalli was appointed to represent the Holy See not just to the government but also to the Catholic Church in France. Resident in Paris, his most regular contact with a senior ecclesiastic was with Cardinal Emmanuel Suhard, Archbishop of Paris since 1940. Suhard had studied at the Jesuit-run Gregorian University in Rome. De Gaulle had a low opinion of Suhard's wartime record, declaring that he had not opposed the Nazi occupation. Roncalli however got on well with the archbishop and relied on his advice on a host of issues.

In his early months, Roncalli read a number of reports compiled by Suhard and other ecclesiastics on the state of Catholicism in France. In particular he was impressed by a book written by two priests, Henri Godin and Yvan Daniel, provocatively entitled *France, a mission country?*

Once described as the eldest daughter of the Church, much of France now had a population which had abandoned the regular practice of their faith. Roncalli had spent two decades in countries where Catholics were in the minority and was surprised at the dramatic collapse of organised religion. From his reading of history he came to the conclusion that the Church had not recovered from the effects of the French Revolution. Even in Paris with its population of five million only a minority of Catholics regularly attended church. He sometimes drew comparisons with the Church in Italy but he pragmatically realised that the history of the two countries was entirely different.

Suhard provided the new nuncio with compelling documentary proof that the Catholic faith in France was ebbing away. The number of vocations to the priesthood and religious life was in steady decline. Suhard had already proposed a new form of seminary in Lisieux in 1941. The following year the college opened to receive seminarians. Here students were not simply assigned to their home diocese but to places of special need throughout the country.

Suhard had devised a novel method of catechising the people. There was little point in urging Catholics to return to the church. Already during the war years a number of priests had entered the work force. Suhard gave permission to several priests to reside outside their presbyteries and work alongside people in factories and other places. It was a dramatic change for parish clergy but it was seen by some as a daring innovation. While some applauded Suhard's vision others denounced him to Rome.

Roncalli reported on this unusual venture to his superiors in the Secretariat of State, unsure what to make of it all. His conservative temperament recoiled at anything which would denigrate what he saw as the indelible sacerdotal dignity.

For all his personal simplicity, his was a life of privilege. He lived in comfortable surroundings, his meals were invariably good and his clothing was splendid. He now inhabited one of the most coveted nunciatures in the world, served by two secretaries, three religious sisters to administer the house, a valet and a driver. The car which ferried him around France was a luxurious Cadillac. While he worked at his desk he listened to records of opera and classical music in the background, his study often clouded with cigar smoke, a habit he had picked up during his posting in Turkey. His salary allowed him to indulge in his passion for books. Although he rarely visited bookshops, a bookseller regularly supplied him with new books, particularly French novels. Among his bedside reading was Georges Bernanos' *The Diary of a Country Priest* and Paul Claudel's *The Tidings Brought to Mary.*

The nuncio's lifestyle had little in common with his fellow priests who lived with and shared the poverty of many of their parishioners. Some priests had abandoned their distinctive black habits in favour of workers' overalls and their presbyteries for small apartments in public housing. As a consequence Roncalli's daily mail contained regular laments from the faithful who were appalled by the developments.

Roncalli knew that the dress of the priest or his location of work was not the defining part of the priest's identity. While living in Turkey Roncalli himself had worn a black suit, white shirt and black tie for a short period as clerical wear was not permitted by law. As he had remarked to his assistant, Monsignor Angelo Dell'Aqua, in 1939 in Bulgaria, 'What does it matter what we wear over our trousers? What is important is that we preach the word of God.' As a wandering diplomat representing the Holy See, he was an atypical priest out of the normative world of the parish.

Roncalli watched the development of the worker priests which began with six priests in the Parisian suburbs in 1946. Within three years the movement had expanded to fifty throughout France and included diocesan clergy as well as Jesuits, Capuchins, Franciscans and Dominicans.

At the same time, France was experiencing a rebirth in biblical studies. The Jesuits at Louviers and the Dominicans at le Saulchoir published noted journals in the areas of patristics and biblical archaeology. Each year Roncalli attended the opening of the academic year at the Institut Catholique. He followed the development of the Catholic schools and from 1946 was the delegate of the Holy See to the nascent UNESCO.

Roncalli found the adjustment to many aspects of French life both a challenge and an opportunity. Many were mystified as to the reasons behind his promotion to perhaps the most prized diplomatic post and he himself continued to wonder at the real reasons.

Reading French came easily to him but speaking was difficult. Preaching on one occasion in a Parisian church he abandoned his efforts and clambered down from the pulpit. 'I am no good at speaking your language,' he told the surprised congregation. 'I blame my sainted mother as she did not arrange to get me French lessons young enough. Anyway, here is what I wanted to say ...'

Paris was sophisticated and Roncalli came from a rural peasant background. While his peasant witticisms garnered smiles he lacked the sophistication of previous nuncios to Paris. At the endless round of diplomatic receptions, his conversation remained superficial. Launched from the relatively quiet diplomatic missions of Bulgaria, Turkey and Greece to the cultured elegance of France, Roncalli was soon lamenting his change. Writing home to his family, he complained that his workload was enormous and that the city was unwelcoming.

Roncalli continued to help locate soldiers who were still unaccounted for at the end of the war. The International Red Cross cooperated with the nunciature in efforts to identify soldiers and repatriate them. The organisation also provided financial support for the soldiers and their families.

At Christmas 1946, Roncalli developed laryngitis. He was obliged to ask his secretary to read the New Year greeting to the President and diplomatic corps. As he stood by the cleric, Roncalli could not keep himself from gesticulating with his hands and making facial expressions at every sentence to the merriment of the assembled politicians and ambassadors.

Roncalli may have underestimated the impact he was having. Invitations to lunch at the nunciature became treasured occasions. The food was always good and the company excellent. He happily welcomed intellectuals such as Schumann, Bidault, Rollet, Mauriac, Maritain and Claudel. Roncalli was pivotal in arranging the appointment of Jacques Maritain as the French Ambassador to the Holy See. The secretaries ensured that the guests were manoeuvred to have a few moments private conversation with the nuncio before they left. What Roncalli heard on these occasions was often typed in his regular reports to Rome.

At the Vatican, officials often complained about Roncalli's reports. Usually filed late, the nuncio regularly mixed up or misspelled names. Foreign names gave him particular trouble. During an audience with Pope Pius, the pontiff reproached Roncalli for his carelessness and insisted that reports be sent more promptly to the relevant Vatican congregations.

Much to the chagrin of Pope Pius, some traditionally Catholic countries, in post-war Europe, allied themselves with atheistic Communism. The trend was regularly denounced as the betrayal of Christian principles. Already in 1944 the Holy Office had published a document which provided for the excommunication of Catholics who embraced atheistic Communism.

During an encounter with the French bishops on 17 March 1949 Archbishop Roncalli urged the bishops to unite against Communism. When Cardinal Suhard died two months later the worker priests movement lost its patron and protector.

Over the years Roncalli undertook a series of visits to the different regions of France, criss-crossing the country several times, attending civic and religious functions. Most journeys were undertaken for a specific purpose. In September 1945 Roncalli visited German military prisoners at Chartres. In 1947 he accompanied the French Pilgrimage Association on his first of several trips to Lourdes and on 15 August of that year attended celebrations at Puy in Languedoc. He loved historical events and attended the seventh centenary of the Council of Lyon between 12–15 June 1948. He also took part in celebrations in Nantes to mark the canonisation of St Louis de Monfort. In 1949 he attended the celebrations in honour of St Julian and also St John Baptiste de Salle. In 1950 Roncalli preached at the sixth National Marian Congress in Rennes which was attended by three hundred thousand Catholics. In 1952 Roncalli presided at a ceremony at the great abbey of La Chaise-Dieu. The Benedictine abbey of Solesmes, renowned for its Gregorian Chant, was a particular draw for him. In 1952 he was in Avignon for the sixth centenary of the death of Pope Clement VI.

Roncalli was responsible for suggesting candidates to Rome to fill bishoprics. His most important challenge came in the aftermath of Suhard's death in 1949, when he was required to find a new archbishop of Paris. In August of the same year, the Archbishop of Bordeaux, Maurice Feltin, succeeded Suhard in Paris. Feltin's was one of three names submitted to Roncalli's superiors in Rome. The posting assured Feltin of a place in the College of Cardinals at the next consistory which was held in 1953. Roncalli and Feltin developed cordial relations and worked together to protect the interests and independence of Catholic schools.

With the election of Vincent Auriol as President of France in 1947, Roncalli had found an unexpected ally. The president liked Roncalli's jovial demeanor in contrast with his austere predecessor. Roncalli's first and only visit to Africa took place in the spring of 1950, when he spent a month in French-speaking north Africa.

Having filled the office of nuncio to France for eight years, Angelo Roncalli received an unexpected promotion. The elderly diplomat had expected Paris to be his last posting, having settled into the French way of life. Although he may not have fully understood the nuances of the country, he had come to value and appreciate its history and the sincerity of the Catholic population. Mastering the language had been a challenge but he had achieved an adequate fluency.

On 14 November 1952, a letter arrived in the diplomatic pouch. The letter came from the Sostituto at the Secretariat of State, Monsignor Giovanni Montini, the future Pope Paul VI. After the death of Cardinal Luigi Maglione in 1944, Pius had declined to nominate a Secretary of State and so Montini became the pontiff's chief assistant.

Montini explained he had met with Pope Pius that morning. The pope asked him to inform Roncalli that the Patriarch of Venice, Archbishop Carlo Agostini, was dying. In the event of the prelate's death Montini had been instructed to ask if Roncalli would accept the office, which traditionally carried the cardinal's hat.

Roncalli was intrigued at the unexpected turn of events. No rumours of Agostini's health had filtered to Paris so it was not possible for him to gauge how long the Patriarch might linger. In any event Roncalli wrote back to Montini immediately, expressing his hopes for the Patriarch's recovery but his willingness to take his place if the need arose.

Two weeks later Pius XII announced what would be his last consistory. Montini wrote once more to Roncalli informing him that his name had been included in the list of new cardinals. The consistory would take place in the

Vatican on 12 January the following year. It was now certain that Roncalli's time as nuncio in Paris was over. However, as Agostini was still alive, Venice was ruled out.

Roncalli speculated that Pius had thought of another diocese in Italy. The bishops of the various Sees, as far as he could tell, were in robust good health. Where could he go now? It seemed that a post in the Roman Curia awaited, perhaps as a Prefect of a Congregation. But his mind was taken from the impending honour by a visit home to his sister Ancilla who was seriously ill with cancer.

Back in Paris he received congratulations from bishops and politicians alike as he awaited news of his final destination.

CHAPTER SEVEN

'LA SERENISSIMA'

Angelo Roncalli's uncertainty came to an end with the death of the Patriarch of Venice shortly after Christmas 1952. With characteristic humility he noted in his diary that he had prayed for the soul of the Patriarch and he prepared to take up his cross and go to Venice. Yet he was proud of the honour which Pius had shown him.

Appointing his successor, Archbishop Paolo Marella, Pius warned him to stay in the nunciature and not spend his time wandering around France. It was an unfair criticism. During his eight years in France Roncalli had visited all but two of the eighty-one dioceses. Pius often told his nuncios that they were to be the hands, ears and mouthpiece of the pope. Roncalli mischievously added that he was also his legs.

Roncalli was above all a pastoral priest. He enjoyed meeting people. He could not stand being locked up in the confines of the nunciature or endure the interminable rounds of embassy receptions. He was voluble and enjoyed recounting episodes and jokes, often at his own expense. Some of his interlocutors found that he was excessively talkative and not a particularly good listener. A Jesuit visitor to the nunciature noted that Roncalli prattled on without saying anything of note. His dislike of confrontation, the Jesuit noted, led him to change contentious subjects to more genial topics.

All the priests Roncalli had admired in his life were deeply engaged with people and little interested in writing up reports to be filed in archives. In particular, Roncalli's episcopal mentor, Radini-Tedeschi, had been at heart a parish priest.

President Auriol invoked a privilege of the former monarchs of France and conferred the red biretta himself at the presidential residence on 15 January. It was unusual to invoke the now defunct custom but it was a sincere tribute that the new cardinal had been truly appreciated and admired in France.

One curiosity remained. It was still unclear where Roncalli was going. Although Montini had indicated that Venice was on offer, it was theoretically possible that Pope Pius might change his mind. Official word had not come as to his final destination. To mark the departure of the nuncio, Cardinal Roncalli was enrolled in the ceremonial Légion d'honneur.

By accepting the ceremony at the presidential palace, Roncalli had missed out on the colourful pageantry in Rome as well as the gossip. The consistory was only Pius' second and, in the event, his last. Twenty-four cardinals had been created on 12 January 1953. Pius sought to internationalise the college and only ten of the new cardinals were Italian.

Official word of his appointment to Venice came in a letter from Pope Pius on 12 January 1953, the very day of the consistory at the Vatican. The venerable history of Venice appealed to the historian in Roncalli. In reality, Venice was arguably the least important of the Italian cardinalatial Sees.

There was little time for the new cardinal to make his farewells. He was somewhat sad to leave France and Paris in particular. Despite his complaints of being overworked he knew that these had been productive and relatively happy years. At seventy-one retirement to Sotto il Monte had been his intention. The house had been made ready. Now his new residence was to be beside St Mark's Basilica, a stone's throw from the lagoon.

Venice

Cardinal Roncalli chose Sunday, 15 March for his solemn entrance into Venice and taking possession of the cathedral of St Mark.

The city was hung with garlands. A large flotilla of gondolas went to greet the Patriarch as his gold and red barge turned into the lagoon. Youths dressed in medieval costumes threw ribboned banners in front of him as the Patriarch stepped on to the pavement outside St Mark's. A large procession of musicians playing brass and timpani accompanied the cardinal and his entourage to the basilica. The train of his scarlet silk cappa magna was carried by a bearer. A white ermine cape covered his shoulders.

The Venetians were delighted to receive a prelate of such note. A man who had worked in the East would certainly understand the bridge between the Catholic and the Orthodox worlds which made Venice unique. That Roncalli came from Bergamo was a mark in his favour as Lombardy and the Most Serene Republic of Venice went back centuries in history. To mark his elevation, the Patriarch added the lion of St Mark to his coat of arms. For Roncalli the echos of his former life continued to resound. His years in Constantinople had helped him develop an understanding of the mystery and ethereal nature of the Orthodox church and her sublime liturgy.

Angelo Roncalli's years in Venice were among the happiest of his life. In his diary he records again and again his contentment at being home among his own people. The house assigned to the Patriarch, to the left of St Mark's cathedral, was somewhat gloomy but he soon made it his home. The central heating did not work and made the winters almost unbearable. Two religious Sisters, Pieparola and Primarosa, tended to the house. He employed a factotum, Guido Gusso, who helped him make his way around Venice.

Shortly after his arrival in the city, the Patriarch chose a thirty-seven-year-old priest, Don Loris Capovilla, as his private secretary. A Venetian priest advised Roncalli that Capovilla was too sickly for the task and probably would not live long. 'Then he will die as my secretary,' replied Roncalli testily. In the event, Capovilla was to become a faithful companion for the rest of his life and outlived Roncalli by more than half a century. In 2014, Pope Francis made the ninety-eight-year-old Capovilla a cardinal, a gesture interpreted as indicating the Argentinian's admiration of Roncalli.

Having lived abroad for many years Angelo was now able to reconnect with his family and see them regularly. If he could not visit as often as he wished, he could now telephone. The distance seemed to be much smaller. Cardinal Roncalli spent each August in his beloved Sotto il Monte and each year several nieces and nephews travelled to Venice on 19 March, the feast of his patron St Joseph, to offer him good wishes.

Life in Venice for the Patriarch was not simply a procession of gondolas or sumptuous liturgies. Although regarded as one of the world's most beautiful cities, Venice was not without problems. The city is built on a series of 118 small islands interlaced with a network of canals and bridges. The diocese includes the industrial cities of Mestre and Marghera. Shortly after his arrival in Venice the Patriarch visited Marghera where some workers had perished in an accident.

Speaking with people in the district he learned of the difficult situation of the inhabitants. The fields were gradually abandoned as people sought work in the cities and suburbs. For Roncalli the development was understandable but disturbing. For his first pastoral letter, he acknowledged the plight of so many post-war Venetians trying to adapt to a changing world.

For the first time Roncalli had the assistance of an auxiliary bishop and other diocesan bishops with whom he developed a close working relationship built on trust. He was also called on to preside over the area bishops of the Triveneto and supervise their annual meetings.

Roncalli became a familiar figure in the city. He walked everywhere with a cane and took the public vaporetto boat, usually accompanied by Capovilla. He saluted everybody and had time to stop and speak readily. Of all Patriarchs in the living memory of Venetians, Roncalli was judged the most friendly and approachable. His portly figure, a double breasted overcoat covering his red-piped soutane, and a soup bowl hat with red and gold tassels marked him out as he made his way through Venice.

In late March, Roncalli paid a visit to the Venetian seminary situated across from San Marco beside the church of the Madonna della Salute. He explained to the students that he wanted his first official visit to be to the future priests as they were so important in the life of the parish and the diocese. Roncalli viewed the parish in the traditional terms of the times, where the priest governed everything and where pastoral councils did not exist.

At the end of February 1954 Roncalli began a three-year visitation of all the parishes of the diocese. These excursions lasted no more than a day or two but included Mass in the parish church and a visit to the schools, convents, social centres, homes for the elderly and other parish structures. In addition Roncalli visited the prisons, such as Santa Marta and the Casa Femminile in the Giudecca region. He also visited the hospitals both in Venice and in the surrounding lowlands.

Pope Pius XII had beatified the former Patriarch of Venice, Giuseppe Sarto, who had later become Pius X, in June 1951. On 29 May 1954 Roncalli travelled with a large delegation of Venetians to celebrate the canonisation of Pope Pius X at the Vatican.

For his summer vacation in August, Roncalli travelled as usual to visit his family at Sotto il Monte. On 10 August he celebrated the fiftieth anniversary of his ordination. Rumours had reached his ears that his family and people in the diocese of Bergamo wanted to mark the occasion. On 2 August he had written to his nephew Don Battista, a student for the priesthood. Roncalli told his nephew that he wanted no celebrations as those for his cardinalate the previous year had been quite sufficient. He wished to avoid putting his family to further expense, recalling that his sisters Ancilla and Teresa had died recently. Obedient to his uncle's wishes, Don Battista informed the family. The anniversary was marked with Mass for the immediate family in his parish church in Sotto il Monte at 8.00 a.m. A High Mass was celebrated at 10.00 a.m. and followed by a lunch in the family home.

Roncalli found himself tied to his desk with a number of writing commitments, largely devoted to the pastoral year due to start in September. He travelled to Milan to celebrate the funeral of the Cardinal Archbishop Ildefonso Schuster who had died on 30 August. A month later Roncalli flew to Beirut as the Apostolic Legate for the Marian Year. He had been in the Lebanon some years earlier on a brief visit.

Returning to Italy a week later by ship he disembarked at Brindisi in order to attend the Italian Bishops' Conference meeting in Pompeii. During the encounter he heard that Giovanni Battista Montini had been appointed as Schuster's successor in Milan. Like most others, Roncalli suspected that after thirty years working in the Roman Curia Montini had fallen foul of Pius XII and his supporters. On his way back to Rome Roncalli stopped in Rome to salute his friend and confidant. The two greeted each other cordially but each was embarrassed by the abrupt change in papal favour.

Some of Montini's enemies in the Vatican viewed him as liberal, ready to side with the emerging political left-wing. A split in Catholic Action caused the president of the movement, Marco Rossi, to resign his post. Montini did not inform the pope who wholeheartedly supported the movement. Montini may have hoped that Rossi would reconsider his position. Pius heard of the resignation from other sources and was indignant that he had not been informed by Montini. For many, this explained the promotion upwards and out.

Roncalli, who had been a good friend to Montini, felt the injustice of the move and hoped that Pius might at least make Montini a cardinal. He had lost an influential friend at the papal court and attended the episcopal ordination of Montini in Milan on 12 December. Montini's exile continued to baffle many, as Pius' health had deteriorated. Some doubted that the pontiff would last long and discreet soundings were made for a forthcoming conclave.

Italy in the post-war period

Aided by the Marshall Plan, the Italian economy experienced rapid growth throughout the 1950s. America did not want the expansion of the Communist Party that threatened the fledgling democratic government. The Marshall Plan funnelled some 1.5 billion dollars into the Italian economy between 1948 and 1952. This allowed the country to move from an agricultural to an industrialised economy. Italy was one of the founding member states of the European Economic Community in 1958 which further improved the social and economic situation of the citizens.

As a result of the economic growth of the 1950s large numbers of people from the south of Italy migrated northwards towards the industrialised cities. While the migrants fuelled the growing wealth of the country they also triggered social problems. A vast network of railways and roads were extended to link the metropolitan areas. Housing was erected hastily, often without due attention to the needs or safety of the residents.

The third year of Roncalli's episcopate in Venice was marked by two Missions held in the parishes. The first took place in Venice prior to Easter while the second, at Mestre and Marghera, lasted most of October. They marked a change in organisation from the traditional Missions which consisted of inviting parishioners to listen to sermons in the churches. This time lay people stood on the bridges and corners of Venice and in the public squares handing out leaflets and encouraging people to attend the Mission.

Roncalli was delighted with the success of the Mission. In September of that year he gave a cautious welcome to the Venice Film Festival, marvelling at the new methods of communication but warning of unwelcome developments.

At the annual gathering of Italian bishops in Pompeii in November 1955, Roncalli expressed his concern over gains made by the Communist party in local elections. He had been placed in a difficult position regarding *Il Popolo del Veneto*, a local Christian Democrat newspaper. He received a letter from the Holy Office insinuating that the editor, Wladimiro Dorigo, had Socialist leanings. Although Roncalli defended Dorigo, he wrote in a pastoral letter that year that Catholics were well advised to stay away from 'openings to the left'. Roncalli was under pressure from the Vatican to vocally oppose atheistic Communism and to encourage the people of his diocese to do the same. While it was recognised that Catholics had a free conscience, they were expected to follow the bishop's guidance.

Roncalli announced that the year 1956 would be dedicated to the memory of the first Patriarch of Venice, Saint Lorenzo Giustiniani, who had died five hundred years earlier. Although Venice had been a diocese since 774, Giustiniani had been the first Patriarch. The ancient title was used exclusively in the Latin Church by the Patriarchs of Lisbon and Venice. Roncalli took every opportunity to preach and write about his illustrious predecessor whose relics were carried around the parishes of the diocese.

In his Lenten letter he urged the people to read the Sacred Scriptures for themselves. In the Italy of the 1950s this was an unusual episcopal appeal. Following the sixteenth century, Catholics and Protestants were divided over the primacy of the Word of God or its interpretation according to tradition. Roncalli wanted the people to read the Bible for themselves rather than rely on interpretations.

In March 1956 the Patriarch made a brief visit to Rome to offer congratulations to Pope Pius XII on the occasion of his eightieth birthday. He found the pontiff ailing and confused. The week in Rome gave him the opportunity to catch up with various acquaintances, most of whom felt that the pontificate was veering towards its end. The pastoral year concluded in June and Roncalli spent a long vacation in Sotto il Monte where he remained for almost two months.

In September 1957 Roncalli was invited to address a symposium in Palermo. The occasion was the seventh annual week of study run by the Association for the Christian East. The former diplomat who had spent two decades in the East gave the inaugural address. In his speech he admitted that there were historical faults on both sides resulting in the millennium-long split between the Churches of the East and the West. While he envisioned a return to the unity of the Western Church, he accepted that sacrifices needed to be made on both sides in order for this to be achieved.

Decline of an Offer from Rome

In 1957 the tranquility of Roncalli's Venetian sojourn was disturbed by a message from the Substitute at the Secretariat of State, Monsignor Dell'Acqua, inviting him to leave Venice and take over the role of Prefect of the Consistory. One of the chief duties would be the selection of bishops.

Roncalli was troubled by the unexpected invitation. Dell'Acqua was sounding out the Patriarch's willingness to leave Venice for Rome. Roncalli's episcopal motto was *Oboedientia et Pax,* 'obedience and peace'. For the first time in his life, he declined an offer from Rome.

Roncalli provided three reasons. In the first place he explained that his age – now seventy-six – precluded him from making such a move. Secondly he argued that he was much better as a pastor than a curial official and thirdly he claimed insufficient knowledge of the juridical needs of the Universal Church. Surely, he suggested to Dell'Acqua, it would be easier and more appropriate to find somebody better suited.

Roncalli need not have worried that Pius would have insisted. On 9 October 1958, the nineteen-year pontificate came to an end at the papal country residence at Castel Gandolfo. Pius had travelled as usual in early July to spend the summer months in the palace which had been begun in the seventeenth century by Pope Urban VIII. By now he had been feeble and clearly unwell and many in the inner circle had been awaiting the end of the reign.

The state of Pius' delicate constitution was well known. In his latter years he had entrusted his health to an oculist, Riccardo Galeazzi-Lisi, who had tried out a number of bizarre cures on the papal patient. Pius' condition had deteriorated in early October.

Pius had greatly elevated the status of the papacy. His thin frame and gaunt face were seen as the epitome of a pope who had poured out his life in service of the Church. Most Catholics revered him and admired the undeniable dedication he had brought to this mission.

The death throes of the pope were made public through a series of radio broadcasts from the papal chamber. The elderly pope was racked by hiccups. The Camerlengo of the Holy Roman Church took charge and summoned the cardinals to Rome, firstly for the funeral and later for the conclave. The Camerlango is in sole charge of the administration of the Catholic Church during the sede vaccante, the period between the death of the pope and the election of his successor.

On the morning of 11 October 1958 the Patriarch of Venice took the train from Venice to Rome. A group of well-wishers, including the mayor of Venice, gathered at the carriage. Cardinal Roncalli lowered the window and saluted the crowd on the platform. 'Don't worry,' he reassured them, 'I have my return ticket.'

Chapter Eight

The Conclave

Cardinal Roncalli arrived in Rome in time to participate in the papal funeral at St Peter's Basilica. The cadaver had been embalmed by Galeazzi-Lisi, Pope Pius XII's personal physician, although he was not qualified as an embalmer. The death of the patient was followed by a botched embalming which caused the corpse to deteriorate during the lying in state. To make matters worse, Galeazzi-Lisi had taken photographs immediately following the pope's demise and had sought to sell them to the media.

Following the period of mourning and the elaborate funeral at St Peter's, the cardinals prepared for the conclave. As those living far from Rome arrived, the date for the opening of the conclave was announced for 25 October. The cardinals had two weeks to prepare. Those living in Italy had longer to lay plans to influence the course of events.

Pope Sixtus V (1585–90) had set the limit to the College of Cardinals at seventy. In the intervening centuries that number was seldom achieved. Pope Pius had kept the numbers low by holding only two consistories in 1946 and 1953. As a result, the number of cardinals at the time of his death was fifty-three. In addition, the majority of the cardinals were elderly, many of them in their eighties.

Most days prior to the conclave the cardinals gathered in the Hall of the Consistory at the Apostolic Palace. These meetings were termed General Congregations, during which the cardinals considered a large number of items which had to be addressed as the conclave loomed. Some of the issues were banal, such as the robes each was expected to wear or their living quarters and seating arrangements. Others were concerned with food and dietary requirements. More prosaic were the instructions as to the manner in which the election was to be announced and how the civil authorities were to be informed of and received by the new pope.

After nine days of mourning the cardinals entered the Apostolic Palace to commence the proceedings of the election. Here, in the area surrounding the Sistine Chapel, fifty-one wooden cubicles had been erected. These would be the temporary lodgings of the cardinals until a new pope emerged with two thirds of the ballot. Two cardinals had died immediately following the death of Pius at the beginning of the conclave. Cardinal Edward Mooney of Detroit died of a massive heart attack three hours before the conclave began.

Election by conclave has been required by church law since 1274. For more than two and a half years following the death of Pope Clement IV in 1268, the cardinals, gathered at Viterbo, had failed to elect a new pope. Only when they were confined to the bishop's palace, the roof was stripped and food was rationed, did an election result. Most subsequent conclaves were reasonably rapid affairs and the more recent popes had been elected within a matter of just a few days.

The conclave commenced with the swearing in of the cardinals. Each of the fifty-one cardinals present took an oath to faithfully and conscientiously elect the candidate they thought was the most suitable to become pope. Although technically any lay Catholic man could be elected, not since Urban VI in the fourteenth century had a non-cardinal acceded to the papal throne.

Most conclaves firstly address a fundamental question: Should the cardinals vote for change or rather should they try to elect someone in the mould of the defunct pontiff? No matter how successful a pontificate may have been judged to be, the cardinals generally prefer to take a new direction. Pius' pontificate was accepted as successful, at least until his grave illness in 1954. Some felt that the final years were of regrettable decline.

Most of the cardinals realised that a different approach was needed. Pius said as much when he applied the legendary words of Louis XIV to himself – *après moi, le déluge,* 'after me, the flood'.

The Italians were confident that one of their number would be elected. They accounted for seventeen of the fifty-one cardinals. Although Pius had sought to internationalise the College of Cardinals the Italians still numerically made up the largest block. They were united by their language. Some cardinals from other countries had Italian blood and it was presumed that they would support the Italian candidate. Other Catholic countries had surprisingly few cardinals. France had only six cardinals, Spain had three while Argentina had one.

The challenge for the Italians was to settle on one strong candidate and support him. A number of cardinals emerged as papabile, worthy of election. In the field were Alfredo Ottaviani, Prefect of the Holy Office, Giacomo Lercaro, Archbishop of Bologna and Ernesto Ruffini, Archbishop of Palermo. Giuseppe Siri, Archbishop of Genoa, was considered too young at fifty-two. Some considered Giovanni Battista Montini, Archbishop of Milan. But Pius had pointedly not made him a cardinal and so his chances of serious consideration were slim.

At first, Roncalli was not considered, his name rarely featuring in the pre-conclave discussions among the cardinals. For a start, his age could be problematic. At seventy-six, he was thirteen years older than Pius had been when he was elected. But that could be to his advantage as few cardinals wanted another pontificate of two decades.

The Italians have a saying, 'We want a Holy Father, not an Eternal Father.'

Roncalli was seen at best as a compromise candidate. Lacking the diplomatic skill of Pius, he also lacked his command of languages. The career of the former diplomat was not particularly outstanding, having achieved little of great impact during his three decades in the diplomatic service. Nor had his period of five years in Venice yielded any particular achievements worthy of note. All in all, Roncalli would do, but only in the case of a deadlock.

Perhaps half a dozen cardinals among the fifty-one entering the conclave believed that they would emerge as pope. Roncalli was one of those who had felt the pressure mounting in the last days leading up to the conclave. Many cardinals had indicated that they would vote for him even if he wouldn't be their first choice. Nonetheless it was clear that his name was now emerging as a frontrunner.

The cardinals took their place in the Sistine Chapel. Above their heads was the great fresco of the Creation of the World painted by Michelangelo Buonarotti between 1508 and 1512. Over the High Altar rose the artist's mighty depiction of the Last Judgement. Around the walls were scenes from the lives of Moses and Christ, painted to commemorate the dedication of the chapel by Pope Sixtus IV in 1483. Everywhere were reminders of the serious importance of the cardinals' deliberations and the power of the papacy.

While the cardinals had carefully considered a number of candidates during the two weeks of General Congregations, it was all to play for during the actual conclave itself. Several popes had threatened cardinals with excommunication if they should seek their own promotion or bind one of their number to pacts to be delivered after election to office. Once a name achieved a two-thirds majority, the election was deemed valid.

Speaking off the cuff some months after his election, Pope John gave an insight into the way the election had proceeded. In an audience granted to the students of the Armenian seminary, he admitted that days before the conclave began he knew 'he was in danger'.

By the time the cardinals began to vote just two names had garnered a large number of votes; the Patriarch of Venice and the Patriarch of Cilicia, Cardinal Gregory Peter XV Agagianian. Roncalli colourfully described their names as being like chick peas boiling up and down in a pot.

Four ballots were cast on Sunday 26 October. None were conclusive. After each session the ballots were collected and burned in a stove in the chapel. A long-funneled chimney led out through an opening in the roof. The curious crowd in the Square and those listening by radio or watching on television followed the black plumes as they unfurled into the azure Roman sky.

The following day Roncalli's candidacy was mounting. Several cardinals called to his cell on both evenings and discussed the impending election. Roncalli knew from history that votes could rise but just as sharply fall away. Capovilla noted that Roncalli grew more pensive during the day. That evening the Patriarch ate in his cell rather than joining his fellow cardinals at supper.

The morning session of 28 October all but sealed his fate. Several sources over the intervening years confirm that the Patriarch of Venice now commanded between thirty-two and thirty-five votes. The afternoon was to see him through. As the scrutineers read the ballots they called out Roncalli's name thirty-eight times. Shortly before 5.00 p.m., Angelo Roncalli was elected the two hundred and sixty second successor of Peter.

Cardinal Tisserant, the Dean of the Sacred College of Cardinals, approached Roncalli to ask if he would accept his canonically valid election. Roncalli acceded with a few words. Asked by what name he would be known, the newly elected pontiff replied – *Vocabor Ioannes,* 'I will be called John.'

The choice of name, the most popular name in the papal succession, was controversial for it was also the name of a fifteenth-century antipope. The new pope later recounted that his choice was inspired by his devotion to St John the Baptist. It was, moreover, his father's name.

As the bells pealed the news of the election throughout the city, thousands of people made their way to the Square. When John accepted his election, all the cardinals lowered the canopies over their heads. Only the canopy of the erstwhile Patriarch remained.

The pope had to sign a document confirming the election and was led to the sacristy behind the High Altar where the papal tailor was waiting. As he changed into the white robes the tailor watched earnestly, lest they prove too small. The pope slipped off his black buckled shoes as the red and gold embroidered slippers were placed on his feet. The red velvet mozzetta, trimmed with ermine, was lowered around his shoulders, and over that a gold and red embroidered stole. A jewelled pectoral cross was hung around his neck. Returning to the chapel a few minutes later the pontiff received the obeisance of the cardinals present.

Shortly afterwards the newly-elected pope went to the balcony overlooking St Peter's Square. Pope John XXIII gave his blessing in Latin – *urbi et orbi,* 'to the city and to the world'.

After supper that evening and a short meeting with Cardinal Tardini, the pope decided to retire for the night. The conclave officials realised that they had overlooked preparing a room for the new pope. Roncalli's bed was hastily transferred into the office of the Secretary of State which had been unused for several years.

The next day John took possession of the papal apartments on the uppermost floor of the sixteenth-century Apostolic Palace. The private apartments consisted of a large salon, two offices, a chapel, a dining room, a sitting room, kitchen facilities and a large bedroom.

The bedroom had two windows. One window opened towards Castel Sant'Angelo and the city of Rome. The other overlooked St Peter's Square and the Janiculum Hill. John had a large desk installed between the two windows where he could see St Peter's cupola. Apart from a few excursions, John was to spend the rest of his life within the 108 acres of Vatican City and he would die in this room less than five years later. At Sotto il Monte the Roncalli family listened to the unfolding dramatic events in Rome on a radio which Angelo had given to them years earlier. Excited villagers crowded into the homestead to congratulate his dazed family.

Chapter Nine

The First Sixty Days

On 4 November 1958, the feast of his beloved St Charles Borromeo, John XXIII was crowned with the triple tiara on the loggia of St Peter's Basilica overlooking the piazza. Over one hundred and fifty thousand people crammed into the Square on the wet morning. The five-hour coronation was carried out in Latin and watched by millions on television.

For almost two decades the Catholic Church had been governed by a skilled diplomat. Eugenio Pacelli had trained as a diplomat at the Vatican's academy and both spoke and read a number of languages. Through his years in the Roman Curia he became aware of the strengths and weaknesses of the papal court. Reserved and remote by nature, Pius had fostered a semi-mystical view of the papal office. Receiving heads of state or a group of school children at the Vatican, Pius prepared for each encounter with punctilious care.

In the latter years of his pontificate Pius had drawn the administration closer to himself, dispensing with all but his trusted and known personnel. As he often repeated to his staff, 'what I want is executors, not collaborators'. He had become withdrawn, giving rise to concerns about his mental health. From 1954 onwards he had grown reserved and did little more than make necessary appearances. A Bavarian nun, Sr Pasquelina, had guarded access to the pope, her influence growing as the pontiff's health weakened.

John's arrival to the papacy heralded a notable change. Although he had an equally exalted view of the papal office, his modus vivendi was quite different from that of Pius XII. Having spent almost three decades as a diplomat, Angelo Roncalli's spontaneous nature was to communicate. He enjoyed chatting with people from all walks of life. While the gardeners were required to withdraw when Pope Pius walked in the grounds, Pope John jovially greeted them, inquiring about their work and their families.

Pope John confirmed that Don Loris Capovilla would remain as his private secretary. He had come to trust and like Capovilla and during the pontificate confided in him on almost every aspect of his ministry.

Speaking with the director of the Vatican newspaper, L'Osservatore Romano, the pope asked him to change the traditional phrases such as 'we have learned from the August lips of the Roman pontiff,' or 'the illumined Holy Father'. Instead, John suggested, 'just refer to me as the Pope.'

The papal court retained most of its ornate trappings. When he appeared at ceremonies in St Peter's and the Lateran he was carried shoulder-high on the sedia gestatoria, ostrich plumes waving behind him. The backdrop for colourful liturgies and ceremonies was the great Baroque masterpiece of St Peter's Basilica. As in courts of old each person had their place and these were guarded jealously. Under Pius, access to the papal apartments was severely restricted. John signalled a change on 7 November when he granted a private audience to Roger Schutz, prior of the small ecumenical community of Taizé, along with the subprior Max Thurian. John invited the visitors to sit down beside him, in a breach of strict Vatican protocol; only the highest dignitaries were invited to be seated in the presence of the pope, and protocol did not allow for protestants to be seated beside the pontiff.

Greeting the visitors, John exclaimed in French, 'Ah, Taizé, that little springtime!' The gracious gesture was repeated by Schutz and Thurian when they recounted how warmly they had been received by the pope. The words rebounded throughout the Christian community as a sign of a new era in inter-church relations. Schutz recalled that John seemed like an elderly grandfather enquiring about far-off family members and speaking fondly of his years in France.

A series of audiences were granted to the heads of state who had attended the papal coronation. These were more formal, although John put his visitors at ease as he chatted amiably about their countries and enquired about their families.

In a spontaneous act John visited the Roman cemetery at the Campo Verano on 2 November to mark the Commemoration of the Faithful Departed. Having recited the *De Profundis* and blessed the graves, he passed by the church of San Carlo in the heart of the city centre where he had been consecrated Bishop on 19 March 1925. The unannounced visit delighted the passers-by, and startled the clergy of the church who were unprepared for the visit.

On 21 November 1958 John went to the country villa at Castel Gandolfo where Pius had died a month earlier. This was the first of some 152 excursions, a marked contrast to Pius who rarely left the Vatican during his two decades in office.

On 23 November John took possession of the Basilica of St John Lateran, the cathedral of Rome. The basilica was packed with curious Romans and thousands of well-wishers who wanted to catch their first glimpse of the pope's diminutive figure.

Returning to the Vatican, John stopped to visit San Clemente, the church dedicated to a first-century predecessor and in the care of the Irish Dominican Fathers. He wished to pay homage to the relics of Sts Cyril and Methodius and to underline his appreciation of the spiritual heritage of the Christian East where he had worked for so long. The saints were particularly venerated in Bulgaria.

A week later John returned to the Lateran, this time to meet with the students of the Roman Seminary. 'Everyone calls me Holy Father,' he told the seminarians. 'Well, I want you to pray to the Lord for me that I can be just as holy as they want me to be!'

On 15 December John convoked the first of the five consistories of his pontificate. There were several Metropolitan Sees such as Westminster, Vienna, Naples and Boston, whose archbishops were normally cardinals. John also had to appoint cardinals to head various Vatican offices.

The most pressing appointment was that of the new Secretary of State. At 10 p.m. on the night of his election John had summoned the seventy-year-old Domenico Tardini and appointed him to the position. This office carried the title of cardinal and so Tardini was elevated. Tardini was a curious choice. The two men had not seen eye to eye over a number of issues pertaining to the curia. Tardini may not have had a high opinion of Roncalli but he was loyal to the papacy and knew that the new pope needed his experience and knowledge.

A mark of respect and one which drew the approval of many was the elevation of Giovanni Battista Montini, the Archbishop of Milan. Pius' failure to confer the red hat on Montini was inexplicable. Roncalli esteemed Montini and wished to reward his faithful service. By making him a cardinal he not only repaid years of friendship but also placed him among the cardinal electors at the next conclave.

In November John had appointed Giovanni Urbani, the bishop of Verona, as his successor in Venice. When the pope met him at the consistory he told the fifty-eight-year-old that he wanted to appoint younger bishops and also to widen the international reach of the College of Cardinals. For that reason he went beyond the limit of seventy cardinals imposed in the sixteenth century by Pope Sixtus V.

John was shrewd in his dealings with the Roman Curia. He knew that many did not like his new style but he tried to win their favour. Towards the end of the previous pontificate many in the Curia had felt ignored by Pope Pius. John restored the regular meetings with heads of Congregations and other principal offices. Word trickled down from the Cardinal Prefects that the pope was interested in various aspects and elements of work. Within weeks of his election he appointed a group to examine themes for his encyclicals. Several advisors were chosen from the Curia.

On Sunday 6 December 1959 Dwight D. Eisenhower, President of the United States, was received in audience. It was only the second time a sitting president had met with a pope. John read a brief welcome in English, which the American visitors found difficult to understand, and his pronunciation caused the delegation a deal of mirth.

The Feast of the Immaculate Conception on 8 December celebrates the dogma defined by Pope Pius IX in 1854. Pope John travelled to the Piazza di Spagna to place a garland of white and yellow roses at the base of a statue erected to celebrate the event. Again the Romans packed the streets leading up to the statue. Looking up at the statue Pope John's gaze fell on the palazzo which houses the Congregation for the Propagation of the Faith where he had worked for almost five years in charge of funding the missions four decades earlier.

Getting used to Vatican protocol proved a challenge. Confiding in a young Jesuit, Roberto Tucci, who later became a cardinal, John lamented that the protocol was often suffocating. 'I have nothing against these good noble guards,' the pope said, 'but so much bowing, such formality, so much pomp, so much parading makes me suffer, believe me. When I go down [to the basilica] and see myself preceded by so many guards, I feel like a prisoner, a criminal and instead I would like to be the "bonus pastor" for all, close to the people.'

John was determined to continue the informal style which he had developed in Venice. On Christmas Day he visited the Bambino Gesú, the childrens' hospital partly sponsored by the Holy See on the nearby Janiculum Hill. The pope wanted to visit the children suffering with polio and unable to return home for Christmas. Following two Masses in St Peter's Basilica and the blessing *urbi et orbi* from the balcony, the pope made the short journey by car to the hospital.

To the surprise of the infants, John strolled into the wards and blessed and embraced the sick patients. Unsurprisingly many were confused and thought that the man dressed in a red velvet cape with white ermine trim was a shaved Santa Claus. Two hours after his arrival the pope departed, leaving gifts for the children.

On his way back to the Vatican the pope stopped at another hospital on the banks of the Tiber. At the Santo Spirito hospital, he was welcomed by the Prime Minster of Italy, Amintore Fanfani, who accompanied him to the wards where he greeted the patients.

After lunch at the Vatican with Angelo Rotta, his predecessor in Istanbul and friend of over forty years, the pope received more visitors. A group from Don Gnocchi's residence for people with special needs were followed by boys from the Villa Nazareth, which Cardinal Tardini had founded in 1946 for children orphaned by the war.

By year's end public reaction to the pope was extraordinarily positive and was mirrored in the international press. The memory of Pius' lengthy pontificate was all but eclipsed by the jovial peasant pope.

John in Prison

At 8.05 on the morning of 26 December, a black Mercedes car drew up on the banks of the Tiber. It was little over a mile from the Vatican. When Pope John stepped from the car, he entered the Roman prison of Regina Coeli, euphemistically named in honour of the Queen of Heaven. Greeted by the authorities John was accompanied to the large space where the four wings of the prison met. From here he greeted the inmates, the first pope to do so in eight decades.

There was an almost deafening applause, drowning out the strains of the carol 'Adeste Fideles', from the cohort of inmates assembled for the occasion. The prisoners were astonished at the event. A small altar had been erected in the courtyard. While most of the 1,500 prisoners remained behind bars, several were allowed to approach the pope.

'Since you could not come to me,' John explained, waving his hands in the air, 'I have come to you. So, here we are! I have come to you, you have seen me and I have seen you. I knew you wanted me to come to see you and indeed I wanted the same. Are you happy I came to see you? I have looked into your eyes and I have put my heart beside your heart.'

The pope was clearly relaxed and spoke animatedly to the prisoners. He recounted, almost in an aside, that his own cousin had also spent time in the same prison for poaching. It had happened, the pope told his audience, when he himself was a boy. The official report in the next day's edition of L'Osservatore Romano discreetly omitted to carry this detail.

Concluding his address to the men, he promised that he would remember their wives and families in his nightly rosary. 'I am thinking along with you of your babies who are your pride and your sadness, your wives, your sisters, and your mothers.'

John was accompanied to one wing and to the infirmary. The prisoners in their striped uniforms knelt as the pope blessed them and patted their heads. One wing remained closed to the pope as it contained prisoners the prison authorities judged too dangerous. John asked to visit but was told that no preparations had been made. Returning to the Vatican he arranged for three hundred little cards with his photograph to be sent to the inmates of that wing.

In his diary that night he noted there was 'great astonishment in the Roman, Italian and international press. I was hemmed in on all sides: authorities, photographers, prisoners, wardens'.

The next day at St Peter's the pope ordained eight new bishops. Four were destined for the Roman Curia, one for a diocese and three for the missions. The diocesan bishop was Albino Luciani of Vittorio Veneto who would become Pope John Paul I twenty years later.

Chapter Ten

A Diocesan Synod and an Ecumenical Council

John spent most of January attending to matters of government. It was time to look at the Roman Curia and become acquainted with those who served there. Although he knew some officials from his time as a diplomat, he needed to acquaint himself with the extensive bureaucracy.

Rather than summon the staff to the Apostolic Palace John undertook a series of visits to each of the sixteen congregations, most of which were in or close to the Vatican. The workers and staff were astonished to see the pope walk along the corridors and enter their offices. Word soon went round to make sure that all the offices were tidy in case the pontiff arrived unannounced.

John was as pleased with these visits as were the staff, noting in his diary the cordial and friendly greeting he had received from every member. These were followed by two more surprise visits, to the barracks of the security forces and to the barracks of the Swiss Guards. It was difficult to guess where he would turn up next.

On Sunday 25 January, the Feast of the Conversion of St Paul, Pope John travelled to St Paul Outside-the-Walls. The ancient basilica, which was built in the fourth century over St Paul's tomb had been destroyed by fire in 1823 but had been rebuilt by 1855. It had long been served by a community of Benedictine monks who lived in the adjacent abbey. It was just three months since John's election to the papacy.

Crowds sheltered from the rain in the portico as the pontiff's sedan drew up. This was the pope's first visit outside the Vatican in the New Year. The religious feast had garnered little interest among the Romans and Vatican officials prior to John's election. Recognised as a keystone by all Christian communities, St Paul was the perfect patron of ecumenism. But in the 1950s Catholic ecumenism consisted largely of prayers for the return of heretics to the fold of the Church. Recalling the visits of the 'heretical' King Edward VIII and Kaiser Wilhelm more than half a century earlier, Angelo Roncalli had rejoiced at the change which his experience in Bulgaria, Turkey and Greece had taught him.

The Solemn High Mass lasted almost two hours. Among the prayers included at John's wish was one for the Catholics of China, where there was a credible danger of schism. At one o'clock the pope met the twelve cardinals who had assembled to greet him in the abbey chapter room. The address, expected to be a formal expression of wishes for the unification of the Church, caught most of the seventeen cardinals by surprise.

'Venerable brothers and Our beloved sons. We announce to you, not without a certain emotion, but also with a humble resolution the name and the proposition of a double celebration. It is that of a Diocesan Synod for the City and an Ecumenical Council for the Universal Church.' In addition, he added, the Code of Canon Law, last modified in 1917, would be reviewed and brought up to date.

Writing in his diary that evening, the pope reflected drily on the reception his announcement had received. Rather than a ripple of applause, the cardinals were silent. Although probably stunned at the daring announcement from the 'caretaker' pope, they showed no sign of support.

Pope John recorded his disappointment but his usual optimism shone out as he trusted that the cardinals would gradually come to accept the proposal.

The idea for a General Ecumenical Council, a gathering of bishops and theologians, was not new. Some twenty Councils had been held over two millennia. In 1948 Pope Pius XII had considered convening such a meeting. It would, in effect conclude the First Vatican Council, suspended on 20 October 1870 due to the arrival of Italian troops which sent the bishops scurrying home lest they become caught up in the impending hostilities.

Among Pius XII's objectives had been the clear definition of dogmas in doubt, such as the Assumption of Mary into heaven. The Council was to have been internal, aimed at tightening discipline within the ranks of the clergy and clarifying disputed points in canon law. The Papal Nuncio to Italy, Archbishop Francesco Borgongini-Duca, had prepared the necessary documents for the convocation of the Council prior to his death in 1954. Pius then felt that he was too old to preside over a General Council and had let the idea rest.

John had initially mentioned convoking a Council to Don Loris Capovilla on 30 October, just two days following his election. On 2 November he had noted in his diary that he had consulted some advisors about the idea. On 20 January 1958, he had spoken of the project to Tardini.

The pope realised the importance of Tardini's support and that of the Curia, suggesting that the idea had recently dawned on him and that he was seeking Tardini's advice as Secretary of State. Tardini had already heard from other sources that the old man intended to hold the Council. He acquiesced to the pope's suggestion although he showed little enthusiasm.

John initially thought that the Council would last no more than three months, and would give a glorious exposition of the Catholic faith. If the Council could start in October that year, the Council Fathers could be home by Christmas. It would also provide the various separated Churches the opportunity to see the beauty of the Catholic tradition and perhaps fan a flame to work for unity.

Over the following days several cardinals tried to discreetly dissuade the pontiff from proceeding with the double events. Whatever the merits of a diocesan synod for Rome, there seemed little point in holding a worldwide Council at the same time. Pope John countered that Pope Pius XII had intended calling such a gathering to conclude the First Vatican Council.

John became increasingly stubborn as various curial officials tried to talk him out of the proposed Council. The lack of support irritated him. When some contended that the time frame was unrealistic and that perhaps another pope would have to bring the Council to a conclusion, John countered that Pius IX had been seventy-seven when the First Vatican Council had opened.

Others pointed out that the general situation of the Church was good. Parish attendance was steady and the number of Catholics globally was growing. The work of the missionaries was bearing fruit as the Catholic faith continued to advance in new territories. To the cardinals' advice to maintain the status quo, John retorted that France, to take one example, was in danger of losing the faith entirely.

The cardinals and curial officials realised that this would be no transition papacy. John was determined to leave his mark and nothing more daring than a Council could be imagined.

In March 1959 John took the unusual step of asking Capovilla to find a journalist to whom he could give an interview. This was the first time a pope would speak with a journalist and give permission to publish an account of the conversation. Capovilla contacted Mario Missiroli, editor of the Italian daily *Corriere Della Sera*. John's preference was to find a journalist who would not be overawed at the task of posing questions to the pontiff. The editor suggested Indro Montanelli who was an avowed atheist. John expressed his approval and an interview was set up to take place in the papal apartments the following month.

John spoke at length about his life prior to election and the changes to his life since the beginning of the pontificate. In the course of the conversation John mentioned the Council several times. Montanelli reported faithfully how important the forthcoming Council seemed for John. The interview, published on page three of the newspaper, revealed to the general Italian public the pope's intentions.

John's words sparked off a debate in Italian society which was soon transmitted globally. It was poorly received by a number of cardinals who were dismayed that the mystical vision of the papacy carefully constructed during Pius XII's nineteen-year pontificate was being so cavalierly dismantled by the smiling peasant pope.

Cardinal Giuseppe Sarto, Patriarch of Venice, had quipped as he left to participate in the conclave of 1903 that he would return from Rome dead or alive. Elected Pope Pius X, Sarto was unable to fulfill his promise. Roncalli had hoped to bring the body of the pontiff, who had been canonised in 1954, to Venice but had failed. Now as Pope John he authorised the return of the body to Venice on a month-long visit.

On 10 April 1959 the crystal and metal sarcophagus was placed on a train at the old station at the Vatican. The pope, several cardinals and Vatican officials boarded the carriage just before it departed on its journey to Venice. John had mixed feelings about political and theological aspects of Pius' pontificate but he had no doubts concerning Pius' sanctity.

By early summer John had put his plan into place. On Pentecost Sunday, 17 May, John established a preparatory commission under the care of Cardinal Domenico Tardini. Most cardinals continued to harbour grave doubts about the enterprise.

Curial officials were relieved at Tardini's appointment. They preferred to have a member of the Curia steer the Council rather than an independent commission made up of experts. John knew the cautious curial mindset and its aversion to change. Accordingly he appointed a number of non-curial bishops from different parts of the globe. Speaking with Tardini, Pope John recalled that after the Second World War three great institutions were born. All three – the United Nations, the World Food Organisation and UNESCO – were American but had become international. John asserted that the Church had more to give and should foster dialogue within the structures of the global Church. It was difficult to argue with John's optimism.

In advance of the Council the preparatory commission contacted bishops throughout the world, requesting them to respond to a questionnaire which was dispatched on 18 June. Ostensibly the document was to elicit information which would be used in compiling a set of issues to be discussed on the Council floor. More than two and a half thousand bishops were invited to take part along with a group of theologians and experts on subjects the Council was due to consider.

Eight months into his pontificate, on the Feast of St Peter and Paul, 29 June, Pope John published his first encyclical, *Ad Petri Cathedram*. The central themes were Truth, Unity and Peace. The document contained an avuncular warning of the dangers of modern life. It had little of the benign outlook which was to mark later documents as it was ghostwritten by theologians who failed to understand John's vision. Given that the new pontiff was gradually finding his way this was understandable, although not a mistake which he was to repeat.

A second encyclical followed just a month later. Published on 1 August 1959, *Sacerdotii Nostri Primordia* celebrated the centenary of the death of St John Vianney. Roncalli had warm memories of a visit to the French village of Ars where Vianney had been a noted pastor and confessor.

On 5 September 1959 Pope John held a General Audience, the first of eighteen which he gave over the course of his pontificate. On 25 August John left Castel Gandolfo on a day-long excursion to two shrines at Genazzano and Bellegra. The meeting was for the sixth Congress of the Association of Catholic Teachers of Italy and he recalled fondly his own pastoral experience of working with young people more than half a century earlier in Bergamo.

Today people have become used to regularly seeing the popes at first hand. Pope Paul VI and Pope John Paul II undertook a vast number of papal visits. These journeys made the pope a familiar figure to an increasing number of people across the globe. In addition, recent popes have welcomed people from all over the world to weekly General Audiences at the Vatican. In advance of the Jubilee Year of 1975 Pope Paul VI commissioned an Italian architect to design and build an auditorium where up to eight thousand people could attend audiences. Where the numbers exceeded this space, St Peter's Basilica or Square hosted the meetings. For John, the General Audiences were occasional affairs held only a few times a year.

A third encyclical, *Grata Recordatio*, arrived on 26 September. John wrote that one of his pleasant recollections was of annual letters which Pope Leo XIII wrote in the month of October. Roncalli took up the theme, adding his concerns for mission territories. He concluded with an appeal to young people to embrace the missionary way of life by leaving their homes to spread the Gospel. This was as priests or religious, not as lay people.

On 11 October John followed up the invitation to young people to become missionaries. Presenting crucifixes to a large group of missionaries in St Peters he urged them to travel to new lands to spread the gospel. That afternoon the pope visited the North American College on the Janiculum Hill to celebrate the centenary of the seminary. Pope Pius XII had blessed the complex during a visit on 14 October 1953.

A second General Audience took place on Wednesday 28 October 1959 to mark the first anniversary of John's pontificate. He began the audience by quoting Pope Gregory (590–604) who described the pope as the *servus servorum Dei*, 'the servant of the servants of God'. He expressed his satisfaction with the upcoming Synod and the early responses for the Ecumenical Council. He could also have reviewed the almost ecstatic manner in which the first year of the pontificate had been viewed by most Catholics. His open and gregarious manner had won many admirers. To his delight faithful Catholics from Communist China had sent a beautiful altar to commemorate the anniversary.

Just two years earlier the Chinese government had sponsored the formation of the Chinese Patriotic Catholic Association, which rejected the authority of the Holy See and appointed its own government-approved bishops. This development had been roundly condemned by Pope Pius XII in his encyclical *Ad Apostolorum Principis,* published just months before his death.

John returned to the theme of the missions in an encyclical, *Princeps Pastorum*, published on 28 November 1959. In it he appealed for a native hierarchy and priesthood. The church had been long dominated by its

Middle Eastern and European heritage. A new alignment was needed which reflected the rapid expansion of the church in the previous century.

The Diocesan Synod

The Roman synod continued to play on John's mind and he followed the preparations carefully. In his notes from the annual retreat for the pope and the Roman Curia held at the Matilde Chapel of the Apostolic Palace, he reflected on the mediations preached by Monsignor Giuseppe Angrisani. At meal times Don Loris Capovilla read extracts to him from the letters of St Bernard to St Eugenius II. 'Certain things did not redound to the honour of the Roman clergy in the twelfth century and still survive today. Therefore "one must watch and correct," and bear in patience,' he noted in his spiritual diary.

John celebrated the New Year with some of his nieces and nephews who had travelled to see him. He arranged their accommodation and meals and in the afternoon received them in his private apartment. He was anxious to hear news of the family. He had pointedly avoided granting the family any honours by which previous pontiffs had enhanced or enriched their relatives. As ever, the family brought gifts of cheeses, meats and home-made pasta from his native village.

On 5 January 1960 John gave an audience to the Polyglot Academy of the Sacred Congregation for the Propagation of the Faith in the Hall of Benedictions above the atrium of St Peter's. It provided him with a trip down memory lane. He recalled how on that day fifty-nine years earlier he had attended the chapel of the offices of the Congregation at Piazza di Spagna. It was the first time that he had seen so many people from all over the world, noting their skin colour and the variety of languages. Each dressed in the ecclesiastical uniform of their seminaries or congregations, the young clerics and sisters represented the vigorous spread of the Catholic faith in mission territories.

Two days later, on 16 January, John travelled to the basilica of St John Lateran to open the Diocesan Synod. Such traditional assemblies of clergy with the bishop were designed to confront issues of the day and reappraise the government of the diocese. Some saw the Synod as a forerunner to the Council. John announced to the assembled cardinals, bishops and clergy that due to inclement weather future sessions would be moved to the Hall of Benedictions at the Vatican.

Two weeks later the Synod concluded. In response to an address by Monsignor Luigi Traglia, Vice-regent of Rome, John expressed his satisfaction with the outcome and approved the promulgation of the decrees.

The results of the Synod were a reassertion of the manner in which the diocese had hitherto been administered. Priests were advised to dress soberly in clerical attire, refrain from attending public entertainments and dedicate themselves entirely to their 'flock'. Clerics were to shave the crown of the heads with the traditional tonsure. The distinctive character of the priesthood was underlined. Infants were to be baptised as soon as possible following birth. The liturgy was to remain entirely in Latin and Gregorian Chant was affirmed as the most desirable form of music. Concerts and applause were forbidden in church as was the selling of artifacts, including religious items. Altars were to face east and those facing towards the people were permitted only in exceptional circumstances. Women were forbidden to enter the sanctuary. Seminarians were urged to devote themselves to their studies and prayer. There was little acknowledgement that the world was changing rapidly and in a manner that nobody could foresee.

Chapter Eleven

Preparing for the Second Vatican Council

With the Synod successfully concluded, John shifted his attention to the Council. In mid-March he received the German Jesuit Augustin Bea, former rector of the Pontifical Institute for Biblical Studies. Bea had been a cardinal since December 1959 and was to become an important ally as John pushed forward the idea of the Council. The two discussed the problem of convincing the Curia to pay attention to the expectations of other Christians who were open to advances along the path to restore unity.

On 28 March 1960 John held a consistory to create seven new cardinals among whom was Archbishop Laurean Rugambwa from Tanzania, the first African cardinal. Three cardinals were created *in pectore* whose names were never made public. John was the only person to know of their existence. Occasionally the identity of cardinals was not revealed in cases where their lives might be in danger, as in countries where the Catholic faith was persecuted.

On the vigil of Pentecost, 5 June 1960, John expanded the Preparatory Commission. Over the course of the previous year 2,821 bishops and religious superiors had been consulted. Of that number 2,150 had responded to the questionnaire. To allay fears in the Roman Curia that the Council would be hijacked by 'foreign' bishops or theologians, John shrewdly appointed the Cardinal Prefects in charge of each area that the Council intended discussing. This ensured that the cardinals and their staffs would take ownership of the progress of the Council.

By now John had discovered to his disappointment that the Council would take much longer than he had first anticipated. The hope that the bishops would be home within three months seemed unrealistic. Although resigned to the fact that he might not live to see the Council finished, John was determined at least to inaugurate it.

Despite John's popularity, many complained that the whole Council was to be made up of bishops with only a few male theologians. Among the sharpest critics were the Swiss theologian Hans Küng and the Archbishop of Paderborn, Lorenz Jaeger. There was no place for women or indeed the lay faithful. The pope listened to the suggestions from various quarters and pondered what to do.

The Council had caught the imagination of much of the Catholic world. There was a belief that John wanted to reunite the Christian Churches. In order to give the reformers an appropriate welcome and forum as the Council approached, John established the Secretariat for promoting Christian Unity, appointing Cardinal Bea as its president.

The gentle-spoken seventy-eight-year-old Bea immediately set about winning friends and inadvertently irritating enemies. He had lived in Rome since 1923 and knew the ecclesiastical scene well. He had served for a period as confessor to Pius XII and had contributed to the seminal encyclical on biblical studies *Divino Afflante Spiritu* published in September 1943. Bea submitted the names of a number of international theologians to his new commission, most of which John approved. In his public utterances the mild-mannered German referred to Christians who were not Roman Catholics as 'our separated brethren'.

This infuriated the seventy-two-year-old Cardinal Alfred Ottaviani, custodian of the Faith at the Holy Office who regarded most non-Catholic Christians as heretics.

There was consternation during the Good Friday ceremonies at St Peter's when one of the Prayers of the Faithful referred to the 'perfidious Jews'. The prayer had been modified by John that year. He interrupted the service and requested that the new formula, which omitted the word 'perfidious', be read. The Latin word simply meant without faith, but it also had an underlying meaning of treacherous or untrustworthy. John was anxious that no possible offence be caused.

John returned to the recent Roman Synod with which he had been so pleased and cited its perceived success as a blueprint for the Council. The decrees of the Synod were published and the Vicar of Rome was entrusted to implement them. Preaching at Mass in St Peter's Basilica on 29 June the pope reminisced about the initial reaction to the Synod.

'From time to time, as We gave thanks to God, We have enjoyed recalling with a smile some of the good-humoured remarks that had reached Our ears, declaring in prophetic tones that the escapade We were planning – an undertaking like that of a Synod in Rome – was imprudent from the very first announcement.' In the event, the Synod had little lasting effect on the diocese of Rome.

With the onset of the summer heat many Vatican offices were reduced to a skeleton staff. John moved to Castel Gandolfo in July where he continued to follow the preparations for the Council. Prior to his departure he dispatched Monsignor Carlo Maccari to examine extraordinary stories of a Capuchin friar, Padre Pio of Pietrelcina. It was claimed that for several years he had suffered with the stigmata, wounds similar to the crucified Jesus. Complaints had been made to the Holy Office by some who saw the whole affair as a sordid manner of making money for the rural shrine. Maccari's eventual report sided with the sceptics.

During John's time in Castel Gandolfo the routine of work continued as at the Vatican. He regularly received visitors to discuss the logistics of the Council. Cardinal Tardini continued to keep the pontiff informed, although he irritated John with his persistent negativity. There was little John could do because it was at his insistence that Tardini had accepted his posting as the pope's chief advisor.

On the morning of his return to the Vatican on 23 September 1960 Pope John visited the Benedictine abbey of Subiaco in Umbria. John had last seen the monastery, where St Benedict had begun his monastic life in the fifth century, during a visit fifty-five years earlier. Meeting the assembled monks and nuns he entrusted the Council to the prayers of the enclosed orders throughout the world.

The early autumn was filled with audiences granted to monarchs and political figures. Among the royalty received at the Apostolic Palace with honours were Bhumibol, the King of Thailand, Francis Joseph II of Liechtenstein, Queen Giovanna of Bulgaria, whose parents Roncalli had known during the 1930s and King Gustav VI Adolf of Sweden. The politicians included Willy Brandt, Mayor of West Berlin, Seán Lemass, Taoiseach of Ireland and Harold Macmillan, Prime Minister of the United Kingdom, among others.

The ecumenical aspect of the Council continued to gather momentum and soon bore fruit. On 2 December 1960 Dr Geoffrey Fisher, the Archbishop of Canterbury, was received in private audience at the Vatican. Several cardinals cautioned the pope that Fisher was a Freemason and thus should not be entertained. Ottaviani was incensed that the pope had shown Fisher such cordiality. It was the first time in four centuries that Rome and Canterbury had made fruitful contact.

Although the conversation was superficial it was the beginning of an ecumenical encounter which would soon make visits between pontiffs and Archbishops of Canterbury the norm. Neither the Anglican delegation nor the Secretariat for Promoting Christian Unity wished to overplay the importance of the meeting as there were opponents to rapprochement both in Canterbury and in Rome. Tellingly no official photographs were taken.

John made his annual retreat in the Matilde Chapel between 27 November and 3 December 1960. Eighteen cardinals and fifty-five prelates listened to the meditations preached by Monsignor Pirro Scavazzi. Examining his conscience, John reflected on his many faults and failings. Quoting from Alessandro Manzoni's novel *The Bethrothed,* he confessed in his diary, 'What little I know about myself is enough to make me feel ashamed.'

At Christmas the pope celebrated three Masses. The first was at midnight on Christmas Eve with the diplomatic corps in the Consistory Hall. The next day he celebrated Mass in the Pauline Chapel beside the Sistine Chapel before Pontifical High Mass in St Peter's. Following the Mass, John donned the triple tiara to give the annual Christmas blessing from the loggia of St Peter's overlooking the Square. On 25 December John issued the papal bull convoking the Council.

After a few days' break, on 1 January 1961, the pope celebrated Mass for the International Congress of the Pueri Cantores, the association of children's liturgical choirs.

Turning Eighty

As each year passed, John settled more into the papal office. The papal year was marked out by liturgical feasts and ceremonies. It was now evident that John's global appeal lay not in his formal pontifical acts but in the warmth of his personality. He had an impish sense of humour. Asked on one occasion how many people worked in the Vatican, he paused thoughtfully for a moment. 'I would say about half of them!'

When Queen Elizabeth and the Duke of Edinburgh visited the Vatican on 5 May 1961, John received them in the Apostolic Library. He rehearsed his speech several times, aware that the English-speaking world would be watching closely. He was also conscious that the monarch was Supreme Governor of the Church of England and that the meeting had important ecumenical overtones.

Having read the brief address, he engaged in a colloquial conversation with the young queen. 'Just think what my parents would say if they could see me now talking to the Queen of England!' He asked the Queen the names of her children. 'How lovely it is to hear a mother say the names of her dear children.' On 15 May John published his encyclical *Mater et Magister* which dealt with a number of social themes such as health care, housing and education.

On 30 July Cardinal Tardini died of a heart attack at the Villa Nazareth, the orphanage he had founded in 1946. Two weeks later, on 12 August, John appointed his contemporary Amleto Cicognani as Secretary of State, Governor of Vatican City State and President of the Administration of the Patrimony of the Apostolic See. Cicognani was better disposed towards the Council than Tardini.

Now in the high summer, there was little that could be done until the traditional vacation period for Romans had ended at the beginning of September. During August John decided to spend five days in complete silence to observe the anniversary of his ordination to the priesthood fifty-seven years earlier. At 5.45 on the morning of 10 August he was already dressed and reading his breviary on the terrace of Castel Gandolfo, overlooking the volcanic lake of Albano. Soon to become an octogenarian, he looked back with nostalgia on the years gone by. His focus, however, was on the position he occupied and in particular on leading the forthcoming Council.

On 10 September John broadcast a radio message appealing for peace. The Premier of the Soviet Union, Nikita Khrushchev, spoke well of John's message. In his diary entry on 20 September, John noted that this was the first time a Russian politician had expressed positive sentiments regarding the papacy. He hoped that this would be the prelude to improved relations. John was aware that many Catholics suffered persecution in Russia. While Popes Pius XI and Pius XII had been emphatic in their denunciations of atheistic Communism, John condemned the system rather than the individual adherents.

Various celebrations were planned around the pope's eightieth birthday. These began as he marked the third anniversary of his election on 28 October, and continued until the end of November. The students of the missionary college, the Urbanianum, were received by the pope in audience and performed a concert of sacred music. Several family members and friends travelled to Rome from Sotto il Monte and the Bergamo area. These were lodged in religious houses. On the day of his birthday, the pope invited them to a lunch in the Apostolic Palace. To his particular surprise and pleasure, among the birthday greetings was a telegram from Premier Khrushchev.

As Christmas approached, it was time to prepare the season's greetings. Writing to his brother Zaverio, nicknamed Severo, on 3 December, John recalled the nostalgia the visit of family members had caused. He apologised for not writing more often in the first three years of his pontificate. In the letter he asked Severo to share his greetings with his siblings Alfredo, Giuseppe and Assunta, his sister-in-law Caterena, Severo's wife Maria and other members of the large family. This was the first time in that period, he told his brother, that he had returned to using the typewriter. 'I used to enjoy typing so much and if today I have decided to begin again, using a machine that is new and all my own, it is in order to tell you that I am growing old.'

It was true. The 'fuss' of his eightieth birthday had made him realise his human frailty. For the first time he noted pains in his bones and the sensation of slowing down. Although he admitted to Severo that his papacy had propelled the family to international fame, he maintained that 'what is most important is always to keep ourselves well prepared for a sudden departure'.

John explained why he had never enriched his family as some previous popes in history had done. Born poor, he wanted to die poor and he believed his relatives should do the same. He concluded the letter with thoughts about his parents as well as the members of the family who had died. The names were so familiar. Their brother Giovanni and sisters Teresa, Ancilla, Maria and Enrica. A special thought went to their uncle Zaverio. But the final blessing was to the innumerable children of the family. 'What a wealth of children, and what a blessing,' he concluded before signing his name, Joannes XXIII P.P.

The early months of 1962 were almost entirely taken up with preparations for the Council, which was due to begin in October. There could be little complaint about the amount of work done to date and the consensus achieved. Seventy-two *schemae*, or draft documents, had been prepared by the preparatory commission on a variety of issues.

On 19 March 1962 John held his fifth and final consistory, at which ten cardinals were created. Among them was Léon Joseph Suenens, who had been appointed Archbishop of Mechelen-Brussels the previous November. The visit was to have been a simple courtesy call. The new cardinal took the pope by surprise by his severe critique of the preparations for the Council.

Suenens argued that the amount of work already submitted would effectively drown the efforts at renewal. John listened carefully and found himself in agreement. Suenens warned him that the Council could do more harm than good by building up expectations which were unlikely to be fulfilled.

John asked Suenens to send him a memo with suggestions on how to simplify the proceedings. He also requested that Suenens speak with other influential cardinals such as Montini of Milan and Liénart of Lille. Suenens sent his plan at the end of April.

In the memo, Suenens suggested drastically reducing the number of *schemae*. Several issues could be referred to the Commission for the Revision of Canon Law or permanent post-conciliar commissions. There was no need to waste time on these minor issues on the Council floor. Suenens hinted that the Curia wanted to procrastinate and concluded with the suggestion that greater power be given to local episcopal conferences.

John was greatly heartened by Suenens' suggestions and ordered their implementation. The bishops and theologians had been consulted and their views and suggestions were incorporated into the documents. John insisted on reading the *schemae* drafts.

John made little effort to keep abreast with contemporary theology. He preserved the simple, uncritical piety of his youth. During his pontificate he did not read the works of any of the emerging theologians and was largely unaware of the developments of ecumenical scholarship.

As he worked through the *schemae* John became increasingly irritated. He realised the value of Suenens' plan. The drafts, now preserved in the papal archives, show pencil marks crossing out passages and marginal notes requesting the ghost writers to be more positive in their proposals. For the pope the drafts were indicative of the way in which the curial commissions wished to direct proceedings from Rome.

The pope examined the list of the various experts which populated the commissions and found not only cardinals who were less than well disposed to the Council but also their protégés and trusted collaborators. John's way of overcoming this imbalance was to ask bishops and nuncios throughout the world to recommend theologians and experts who could also be appointed to the commissions. On 20 July invitations were sent to various Protestant and Orthodox bodies inviting them to send observers to the Council.

Prior to his summer vacation at Castel Gandolfo, John began to feel unwell. He noted his weight loss, and felt listless. He had also suffered haemorrhaging and had reduced the frequency of his public appearances. Hoping that the summer break would do him good, he mentioned his discomfort during his monthly visits with his doctor. There seemed little reason for alarm as initially it was thought the pain might be caused by a stomach ulcer. Accordingly John began to take medication to neutralise the effects of an ulcer. Meanwhile on 6 September he published a list with the names of the ten heads of commissions for the Council along with regulations governing the procedures.

The discomfort continued through the summer. Observers noticed how much weight he had lost, in particular from his face. He was clearly unwell. On 23 September 1962 John underwent an X-ray. The diagnosis showed an advanced stomach tumour. Two of his siblings had died with similar ailments and John knew what was in store. He forbade the news to be made public as he did not want his illness to interfere with the preparation for the impending Council. 'At least', he confided to Capovilla, 'let us pray that I may launch the ship. Another can guide it to port.'

CHAPTER TWELVE

THE SECOND VATICAN COUNCIL AND THE END OF A PONTIFICATE

At 6.30 a.m. on 4 October 1962, a train provided by the Italian State pulled out of the Vatican train station. Pope John was on his way to Loreto to pray for the success of the impending Council. The Prime Minister of Italy, Amintore Fanfani, travelled in a separate carriage. The destinations were the shrine of St Francis at Assisi and the Marian shrine at Loreto, the two most popular sanctuaries in Italy. This was the first papal excursion into the Italian heartland since Pope Pius IX had visited the Papal States in 1857, and the subsequent loss of temporal power. The visit had political overtones as John wanted to acknowledge the efforts of the Italian government, which had invested heavily in the area.

The day-long trip was an enormous success. John recalled his happy days shuttling around Italy, Turkey, Greece and France on trains. Although protocol dictated that the pope and Prime Minister should not meet, John sent a messenger to bring the Premier to his carriage where the two engaged in an amiable conversation.

Fanfani headed a coalition which included Socialists, and John's invitation was interpreted by some as an opening to the Left. In particular Cardinal Siri of Genoa, President of the Italian Episcopal Conference, and Cardinal Ottaviani of the Holy Office vociferously opposed the shift in papal alliance. The American government also viewed with concern John's perceived benevolence towards the various strata of Italian left-wing politics.

Although the train was not scheduled to stop at stations, large crowds had gathered at various towns and the train was obliged to pause. Pope John leaned out the window and addressed a few words to the people. He could not contain his delight at the success of the whistle-stop tour and returned to the Vatican late that night too tired to make an entry in his diary.

A week later, on 11 October 1962, the Second Vatican Council opened at St Peter's Basilica. Some two and a half thousand cardinals and bishops from all over the world attended in the largest gathering the Church had ever seen. It was a colourful spectacle as the clergy in their sumptuous robes filed in the great portico of the basilica as the Sistine Choir sang the Litany of the Saints.

Opening Vatican II

During Mass Pope John preached on the reasons for convening the Council. He had composed the sermon entirely on his own. The first duty, he observed, was to defend and advance the truth, which also required the suppression of errors. The aim of the Council was to serve humanity and seek to restore the unity of the Church. This was to be a pastoral Council. No condemnations or anathemas were to be issued as they had been in the past. John dismissed the pessimistic view of the Council which had found some quarter. 'We feel we must disagree with those prophets of gloom, who are always forecasting disaster, as though the end of the world was at hand.' Progress would come with encouragement and all was to be administered with the 'medicine of mercy rather than the weapons of severity'.

Although lay experts had been appointed to the Council, John and most other bishops felt that the purpose of the discussions was to assist the pastors in better administering the Church. The model of church was strictly hierarchical and clerical. Initially there was little understanding of the central role of the lay faithful.

John was exhausted by the long opening ceremonies. That evening he retired uncharacteristically early. The Romans organised a vigil in St Peter's Square as a spontaneous gesture of gratitude for the Council, not least for the increased business in the hospitality trade. Tens of thousands filed along the Via della Conciliazione in a candlelight procession.

Capovilla informed the pope that large crowds had assembled in the Square and suggested that the pontiff address a few words. John grumbled that he was tired. Moreover, this was not scheduled and no speech had been prepared. Capovilla prevailed upon the pope to address the crowd from his study window. Seeing the crowds, John was surprised and delighted with the large manifestation of support for the Council. Taking the microphone he extemporised:

> All the world is represented here tonight. It could be said that even the moon hastens to be close to us tonight so that from above it might watch this spectacle that not even St Peter's Basilica, in its four centuries of history, has ever been able to witness.
>
> We ask for a great day of peace. Yes, of peace! 'Glory to God, and peace to men of goodwill.' If I asked you, if I could ask of each one of you: where are

> you from? The children of Rome, especially represented here, would respond; 'Ah, we are the closest of children, and you're our bishop.' Well then, sons and daughters of Rome, always remember that you represent 'Roma, caput mundi' – Rome, the capital of the world – which through the design of Providence it has been called to be across the centuries.
>
> My own person counts for nothing – it's a brother who speaks to you – become a father by the will of our Lord ... And so, let us continue to love each other, to look out for each other along the way: to welcome whoever comes close to us, and set aside whatever difficulty it might bring.

As he prepared to give the blessing, John added a few more words.

> When you head home, you will find your children. Hug them and kiss your children and tell them: 'This is the hug and kiss from the Pope.' And when you find them with tears to dry, speak to them a kind word. Give anyone who suffers a word of comfort. Tell them 'The Pope is with us especially in our times of sadness and bitterness.' And then, all together, may we always come alive – whether to sing, to breathe, or to cry but always full of trust in Christ, who helps us and hears us. Let us continue along our path.

First Session of the Council and The Cuban Missile Crisis

John decided not to attend the daily sessions of the Council, leaving the bishops greater liberty to debate among themselves. He was able, however, to follow the discussions on the council floor via an internal television in his apartments.

The first full day of conciliar meetings opened on 13 October. The order of business concerned the confirmation of the presidents of the ten working commissions. To the consternation of the curial cardinals, the French Cardinal Achille Liénart moved that the council adjourn in order for the bishops to examine the proposed candidates. Cardinal Josef Frings of Cologne seconded the vote. Less than ten minutes later the first session of the Council ended in confusion.

After three days of deliberations, the Fathers met once more. The curial domination was ended and bishops from northern Europe played a more significant role.

While Catholics followed the opening days of the Council with interest, world attention was focused on hostilities between the US and the Soviet Union. A year earlier, in April 1961, an unsuccessful military invasion of Cuba by Cuban exiles had taken place. The exiles were funded, trained, armed and transported by the American Central Intelligence Agency with the knowledge of the US President. The US feared the left-wing government of Fidel Castro.

In April 1962 the United States government had placed nuclear missiles in Turkey. These were intended to deter Russia from engaging in war. The First Secretary of the Communist Party of the Soviet Union, Nikita Khrushchev, ordered the positioning of nuclear warheads on Cuba. Construction of a site began in the late summer. When the American military authorities became aware of the Russian plan they proposed an air and sea embargo to prevent the delivery of Russian missiles to Cuban soil.

The Russians reacted with the threat of military action. On 24 October, Khrushchev wrote to President John F. Kennedy condemning the American blockade as unlawful and warning of dire consequences. Three days later an American fighter plane was shot down by a Soviet warship.

President Kennedy wrote to Pope John requesting his intervention. The pontiff responded with a plea to both sides.

> We beg all governments not to remain deaf to this cry of humanity but that they do all that is in their power to save peace. They will thus spare the world from the horrors of a war whose terrifying consequences no one can predict. Promoting, favouring, accepting conversations, at all levels and in any time, is a rule of wisdom and prudence which attracts the blessings of heaven and earth.

On 27 October Kennedy secretly agreed to remove missiles positioned in Turkey and southern Italy in return for the removal by the Russians of missiles on Cuban soil. The thirteen-day stalemate was resolved and the world stepped back from nuclear disaster. To mark his eighty-first birthday John visited the missionary college, the Urbanianum. That day he also met a number of Polish bishops present for the Council, among whom was Karol Wojtyla, the future John Paul II.

On 8 December the first session of the Council ended. After two months the greater part of the work had concerned the liturgy and divine revelation. John expressed disappointment, in his diary, at how little had been achieved. He comforted himself by observing: 'At least the ship has been set to sea.'

Deteriorating Health

John's health was now the cause of public speculation. His face looked gaunt and he found it difficult to move. He no longer walked any distance and took a portable sedan chair within the Apostolic Palace.

To John's delight he received Christmas greetings from Khrushchev and Kennedy. The Russian and American presidents had agreed through the intervention of the political activist Norman Cousins to co-operate with the Holy See in the cause of peace. It was an enterprise destined to continue for years. John had met Cousins and had supported the American-Russian detente.

The year ended with a visit to the children at the Bambino Gesù on the Janiculum Hill. It was a brief encounter, under an hour long as John was tired. The lengthy Christmas liturgies, which included Midnight Mass and the morning blessing from St Peter's balcony to the city and the world, left him exhausted and he remained in his apartment, visited only by close relatives from Sotto il Monte.

The new year afforded John a short respite. After the closing ceremonies of the Council and the Christmas liturgies, the pope took a couple of weeks to rest. New medication required a period of adjustment. However, he continued to work and even made an unscheduled visit to the Church of Santa Maria in Trevi. *Time* magazine, the prestigious American review, named John as the Man of the Year and placed his photograph on the cover in January 1963. It was a dubious honour, as in previous years Stalin and Hitler had also featured with the same accolade.

In an audience with Cardinal Agagianian, Prefect of the Congregation for the Propagation of the Faith, John expressed his hopes for the reunification of the Eastern Orthodox Church and the Catholic Church, which he saw in terms of the Orthodox returning to the Catholic faith.

In early January John addressed a letter to the bishops encouraging them to remain positive. Many had expressed doubts over the direction of the proceedings of the Council and John wanted to assure them of his faith in the outcome.

On 20 January John preached a homily to mark the canonisation of the nineteenth-century Italian cleric, Vincent Pallotti. He appeared at St Peter's again on 2 February when he preached on the Feast of the Presentation of the Lord. By now there was serious speculation in the media about the pontiff's health. John had continued to lose weight and his movements were slow and lethargic.

John's Final Months

On 7 March John received a group of seventy journalists at the Vatican. Among the audience was Alexei Adzhubei, the son-in-law of Nikita Khrushchev. Adzhubei was editor of the Russian newspaper *Izvestiya.* John was informed that he and his wife Rada were present and he invited them to meet him privately. The three, along with a translator, spent some twenty minutes in conversation. Few details of the meeting were leaked but the encounter served to strengthen the cordial relations that John wished to have with the Soviet Union.

John issued his last and most celebrated encyclical, *Pacem in Terris,* on 11 April 1963. It had been prepared for him by some professors of the Lateran University the previous January. It was the first papal exhortation addressed to people of good will, rather than only to Catholics. The document dealt with the complexity of the post-war era, marked by latent hostilities in various parts of the world. It examined the issues of fundamental human rights and the role of government in society. The document was well received and during a General Audience on 23 April John noted his pleasure that so many governments had written to him expressing appreciation for the encyclical.

On 1 May, the Feast of St Joseph the Worker, John held a General Audience in St Peter's Basilica during which he confided the forthcoming Council session to the spiritual protection of St Joseph. He realised that his failing health meant that he was now unlikely to see the next session of the Council, due to begin the following October.

The pope's stubborn determination was evident once more when he received the Balzan Prize for peace, humanity and fraternity among peoples, an award inaugurated by the Italian philanthropist Angela Lina Balzan. The award was conferred in the Sala Ducale at the Apostolic Palace on 10 May by Giovanni Gronchi, the former Italian president. The next day John attended the awards ceremony for the other four recipients of the Balzan prize at the Quirinal Palace. He was the first pope since 1870 to enter the palace, formerly a papal summer residence, but now the official residence of the Italian president. John was feeling very unwell on the morning of the ceremony. Despite his pain he insisted on travelling to meet President Antonio Segni at the palace. The pope was taken ill shortly after the ceremony and returned to the Vatican. It was his last official public appearance.

For the next two weeks the pope was confined to his bedroom on the uppermost floor of the Apostolic Palace. A team of medics was assigned to care for him. On 25 May John suffered a massive haemorrhage and the doctors confirmed that the gastric carcinoma had ruptured the lining of the stomach, leading to peritonitis.

The family was summoned. His sister, brother and nephew, Don Battista, left Bergamo and flew from Milan to

Rome. On 31 May John insisted that Capovilla tell him what was happening. He recalled that it had been his duty to tell his bishop Radini-Tedeschi of his approaching death. Capovilla confirmed that the doctors saw no further hope and that treatment would be withdrawn. All that could be done now was to make the patient comfortable.

It fell to the Belgian Augustinian Bishop Peter Canisius van Lierde, Vicar General for Vatican City, to administer Extreme Unction, the Sacrament of the Sick, to the dying pontiff. Overcome with emotion, the prelate made mistakes in the rite of anointing. John gently assisted him in his task, reminding him of the correct procedure.

The family and immediate members of the papal household took turns in keeping vigil at the bedside as the pontiff was dying. On the first two days of June the cardinals were admitted to the bedroom to take their leave of the pontiff. 'My bags are packed, I am ready to go,' he quipped, weakly.

For several days swelling crowds kept vigil in St Peter's Square below the pope's window. On the evening of 3 June Mass was celebrated on the steps of the basilica. At 7.50 p.m., as the Mass concluded, Pope John XXIII died.

The following day the body of the pope was vested in the red dalmatic and chasuble worn for Mass and transferred to the Sala Clementina in the Apostolic Palace. Here the Curia and other Vatican officials paid their final respects. The papal fanon of white silk and gold thread was draped over his shoulders. A gold mitre had been placed on his head.

The body of the pope was transferred from the Apostolic Palace, through the thronged piazza, to St Peter's Basilica, where it lay in state in front of the High Altar for three days of public mourning. Vast crowds filed down the long aisle to see the pope whom they had come to love. On either side rose the empty wooden seating platforms erected months earlier for the bishops attending the Second Vatican Council. These austere structures were an eloquent tribute to the memory of John XXIII, the Peasant Pope from Sotto il Monte, the Pope of the Council.

Conclusion

Not since the sixteenth century, during the Council of Trent, had a conclave taken place during an ecumenical Council.

For the conservative cardinals such as Siri, Ottaviani and Pizzardo it was imperative to promote one of their own. The progressive cardinals hoped for the election of one who would carry on John's legacy.

Seventy-eight cardinals gathered in the Sistine Chapel on 20 June for the conclave from which the Archbishop of Milan Giovanni Battista Montini emerged the next morning as Pope Paul VI. Montini had achieved fifty-seven of the votes which had split between the progressive Cardinal Giacomo Lecaro, the Archbishop of Bologna, Cardinal Francesco Roberti, the Prefect of the Supreme Tribunal of the Apostolic Chamber and the traditionalist Cardinal Ildebrando Antoniutti, former Apostolic Nuncio in Spain. A small group of influential cardinal 'kingmakers' proposed one or other candidate but surrendered in the face of the rapid support gained for Montini as an acceptable compromise.

Pope Paul reconvened the Council on 29 September. During his homily at the inaugural Mass, the pope committed the Council to Church unity and to continuing John's efforts to make the Church and the contemporary world meaningful to each other.

During the period before the conclusion on 4 December the Council Fathers approved *schemae* dealing with the liturgy and communications. The following year they approved the drafts dealing with ecumenism and the Oriental Churches. During this period the seminal decree *Lumen Gentium* was promulgated which emphasised the role of the baptism of the laity. This shifted the balance of evangelisation from the sole care of missionaries and clergy to the vast body of Christ's faithful.

The final session of the Council, held between 14 September and 8 December, saw a frenzy as various documents were rushed to a conclusion. It was realised that the Council could run out of steam and lose the enthusiasm which it had initially garnered under John's guidance. Documents and constitutions on the episcopate and priesthood, on human rights, on the role of the laity and their place in the Church, on the Bible, on Judaism and on missionary activity were promulgated. Days before the Council ended Pope Paul travelled to Jerusalem with several Council members where he met Athenagoras, Patriarch of Constantinople. Embracing each other in a historical gesture, the two men symbolically lifted the mutual excommunications made over a thousand years earlier.

As the Council concluded, Pope Paul established a Synod of Bishops, national and regional representatives of the world's episcopal conferences, who would convene every few years in Rome. This was a concrete expression of collegiality, the co-responsibility of the bishops of the Church.

The years following the Council were marked with unexpected turmoil. There was a marked exodus of priests from ministry and a sudden decline in consecrated life. Abuses in liturgical practices dismayed a vocal minority which would eventually lead to schism.

The publication in July 1968 of the papal encyclical *Humanae Vitae* on the sanctity of life from birth to death caused a furore when artificial methods of birth control were prohibited in Church teaching. Some years later, in 1976, Pope Paul ruled that women could never be admitted to the priesthood which many saw as an act of exclusion rather than fidelity to traditional teaching.

The Council had given rise to perhaps unrealistic expectations. Despite Paul's missionary efforts, notably through a series of apostolic journeys to India, North America, Turkey, Colombia, Switzerland, Asia, Oceania and Australia, the unity of Catholicism was severely fractured. Various lay apostolates developed where people found a forum to develop their own spirituality which for so long had been the preserve of clergy and religious. The permanent diaconate was restored and for the first time in the Church's history the lay faithful embraced and excelled in various fields of theology. This led to the rapid rise of professional theologians who brought a wider experience and expertise than had hitherto been experienced throughout the Church. At the same time grass-roots relations between Catholics and other Christians slowly grew as ancient animosities were replaced by mutual understanding and respect.

Following the month-long pontificate of Albino Luciani as Pope John Paul I, the Polish Cardinal Archbishop of Krakow, Karol Wojtla, was elected on 16 October 1978 as Pope John Paul II. The fifty-eight-year-old pontiff had lived through the horrors of the Nazi invasion of his country during World War II and the oppressive post-war Communist regime. Although he became instantly popular, with his charismatic character, Pope John Paul brought to the papal office a steely determination to impose order on a Church which he saw in disarray.

During his pontificate of more than twenty-six years, John Paul II criss-crossed the globe in a series of 104 papal trips outside Italy, attracting large audiences wherever he went. Most of these trips were to destinations where no pope had ever visited.

Early in his pontificate John Paul censored a number of theologians, including the Swiss professor Hans Küng, for unorthodox teaching. Turning his attention to Latin America, he persistently criticised the political goals of Liberation Theology, which had sprung up during the late 1960s and 1970s, a viewpoint born of his own mistrust of atheistic Communism which he had experienced first hand in Poland. Only towards the end of his pontificate did he agree that Liberation Theology was an important channel to helping people to live out the Christian message.

For all his charm and charisma, John Paul's efforts to unite people in orthodox harmony had mixed success. He emphatically closed discussion on the ordination of women to the priesthood and comprehensively reiterated the Church's traditional teaching on artificial contraception, homosexuality, abortion and euthanasia.

In the latter part of his pontificate John Paul was vocally criticised for not doing enough to eradicate the sexual abuse of minors by clergy and to punish the perpetrators. A series of media revelations demonstrated that throughout the Church there had been systematic cover up of the abuse of children by clerics and religious and that the Holy See was well informed of the scandal. For the first time in history bishops and others responsible were obliged to resign amid public furore.

John Paul strengthened relations between Catholicism and Judaism and fostered dialogue with various world religions. On three occasions the pontiff invited representatives of world religions to a peace summit in the Umbrian town of Assisi. During his visits abroad the pope met representatives of other religions.

Critics accused John Paul of turning his back on the very Council in which he had participated as a young bishop. Ecumenical relations fostered by John XXIII seemed to experience a setback in 2000 when the Congregation for the Doctrine of the Faith issued a document, *Dominus Iesus,* which asserted that the Catholic Church solely embodied the Christian community desired by Jesus.

When Joseph Ratzinger succeeded John Paul as Benedict XVI on 19 April 2005, the German pontiff attempted to carry on much of John Paul's initiatives. Benedict was personally shy and never relished the massive crowds which energised John Paul. Yet Benedict brought an unparalleled theological and cultural preparation not hitherto witnessed in the modern papacy. Originally a liberal theologian who served as a theological expert at Vatican II, Joseph Ratzinger became increasingly more conservative. Like John Paul he was criticised for seeking to reinterpret John's Council. In a Christmas address to the Roman Curia in 2005, Pope Benedict cautioned against dividing into the pre- and post-Conciliar Church. Reform was always needed along with continuity.

During his eight-year pontificate Benedict tried, unsuccessfully, to reconcile the extreme liberal and traditionalist wings of the Church. Citing age and health as the reasons for his abdication, on 28 February 2013 Benedict resigned in order to allow the appointment of a new pope with more physical and mental stamina. He was the first pope to retire in almost five hundred years. General opinion approved of his decision which led to the election of the first pope from the Americas.

The election of the seventy-six-year-old Argentinian Archbishop of Buenos Aires, Jorge Bergoglio, on 13 March 2013 as Pope Francis saw an abrupt change in papal style. Rather than live in the Apostolic Palace the new pontiff chose to reside in the residence of Santa Marta with other clergy employed at the Vatican. Francis placed service of the poor at the centre of his ministry as Bishop of Rome. His first visit outside Rome was to Lampedusa, a small island off the southern coast of Italy to comfort migrants who had travelled from Africa in search of a better life. Many migrants drowned in tragic circumstances as the boats carrying them capsized. The brief visit, which lasted just a few hours, concentrated world opinion on the fate of the impoverished migrants and the responses of the Italian government and the international agencies. With similar acts Francis showed his care for the poor, while reforming the Roman Curia and resolving financial scandals which had erupted over the previous fifty years.

During the conclave of 2005, Jorge Bergoglio gained a large number of votes. As he watched the votes mount he realised that he could be elected. In that event, he later confided to Cardinal Francesco Marchisano, he considered taking the name John XXIV. It would have been a suitable tribute to a pope he admired and who inspired his own pontificate.